CONSIDERING EMOTIONS IN CRITICAL ENGLISH LANGUAGE TEACHING

Groundbreaking in the ways it makes new connections among emotion, critical theory, and pedagogy, this book explores the role of students' and teachers' emotions in college instruction, illuminating key literacy and identity issues faced by immigrant students learning English in postsecondary institutions. Offering a rich blend of, and interplay between, theory and practice, it asks:

- How have emotions and affect been theorized from a critical perspective, and how might these theories be applied to English language teaching and learning?
- What do complex and shifting emotions, such as hope, disappointment, indignation, and compassion, have to do with English language teaching and learning in the neoliberal context in public universities?
- How might attention to emotions lead to deeper understanding of classroom interactions and more satisfying educational experiences for English language teachers and students?

These questions are addressed not just theoretically, but also practically with examples from college classes of assigned readings, student writing, and classroom talk in which various emotions came into play. Thought-provoking, accessible, and useful, this is a must-read book for scholars, students, and teachers in the field of English language teaching.

Sarah Benesch is Professor of English, College of Staten Island/City University of New York

CONSIDERING EMOTIONS IN CRITICAL ENGLISH LANGUAGE TEACHING

Theories and Praxis

Sarah Benesch

NEW YORK AND LONDON

First published 2012
by Routledge
711 Third Avenue, New York, NY 10017

Simultaneously published in the UK
by Routledge
2 Park Square, Milton Park, Abingdon, Oxon OX14 4RN

Routledge is an imprint of the Taylor & Francis Group, an informa business

© 2012 Taylor & Francis

The right of Sarah Benesch to be identified as author of this work has been asserted by her in accordance with sections 77 and 78 of the Copyright, Designs and Patents Act 1988.

All rights reserved. No part of this book may be reprinted or reproduced or utilised in any form or by any electronic, mechanical, or other means, now known or hereafter invented, including photocopying and recording, or in any information storage or retrieval system, without permission in writing from the publishers.

Trademark notice: Product or corporate names may be trademarks or registered trademarks, and are used only for identification and explanation without intent to infringe.

Library of Congress Cataloging in Publication Data
Benesch, Sarah.
Considering emotions in critical English language teaching : theories and praxis / Sarah Benesch.
p. cm.
Includes bibliographical references and index.
1. English language--Study and teaching--Foreign speakers.
2. Critical pedagogy. 3. Emotions and cognition. I. Title.
PE1128.A2B456 2011
428.0071--dc23
2011040536

ISBN: 978-0-415-88203-3 (hbk)
ISBN: 978-0-415-88204-0 (pbk)
ISBN: 978-0-203-84813-5 (ebk)

Typeset in Bembo
by Taylor & Francis Books

Printed and bound in the United States of America by
Walsworth Publishing Company, Marceline, MO.

CONTENTS

Preface	vii
Acknowledgments	x

PART 1: THEORIES   **1**

1 Introduction, Rationale, and My Social/Emotional History   3

2 Emotions in English Language Teaching: Related Literatures   20

3 Critical Theories of Affect and Emotions   37

PART 2: PRAXIS   **55**

4 Sticky Objects in ELT Classrooms: Hope/Disappointment; Resentment/Attachment   57

5 Revisiting Pedagogy about Military Recruitment: From Indignation to Friendship   76

6 Theory Building with Language Acquisition Students: Metaphors of Embodied Emotions   93

7 English Language Teachers' Emotion Work: Management, Embodiment, and Explicit Teaching   109

8 What Remains: Implications for Critical Teaching
   and Research   130

Notes   137
References   139
Index   144

PREFACE

Introduction

Considering Emotions in Critical English Language Teaching: Theories and Praxis is my attempt to extend the research and teaching agendas of critical applied linguistics to include emotions. This project has led me to discover ways of theorizing emotions and affect critically and to apply those theories to English language teaching (ELT) and learning.

My interest in emotions has a long history in my English language teaching career. I was always aware, even if vaguely, that my and my students' emotions figured in teaching and learning. Even at the institutional and social levels there seemed to be emotional climates affecting life inside classrooms. Yet I set emotions aside while pursuing other interests: the politics of testing; challenging institutional hierarchies that subordinated English language teachers and their immigrant students; critical English for academic purposes; and critical media awareness.

However, though my attention wasn't focused explicitly on emotions, there was a nagging sense that I *should* be taking them into account in my research and teaching. They were obviously integral to classroom events, but, at the same time, fleeting, changing, hard to pin down, maybe a little dangerous or presumptuous to attend to. I was a teacher, not a psychotherapist, so was it even appropriate for me to think along emotional lines? Was I qualified to consider the emotional content of English language learning and teaching?

The literature I read on emotions and English language teaching earlier in my career seemed too narrowly focused on anxiety as a deterrent to language acquisition and did not, therefore, draw me in. Because the affective turn in critical theory did not get going until the turn of the twenty-first century, it did not occur to me up to that time that emotions could be theorized as social constructs, rather than private feelings or cognitive structures, and integrated into research on critical teaching.

One of the challenges of writing this book has been explaining what it was about to those who asked me what I was working on. I'd begin by saying I was writing about emotions and English language teaching, almost apologetically, as if this was not a serious scholarly subject. So I'd next jump in to explain that I wasn't taking up emotions psychologically, but, rather, socially and politically. And I'd add that I was writing about emotions not as static or monolithic, but, rather, as overlapping and moving. Then, if I still had my interlocuteurs' attention, I'd tell them that I was writing about connections between teachers' and students' bodies and minds, drawing on Spinoza, who said Descartes got it wrong when he split mind and body. Finally, I'd explain that I was applying theories about emotions to English language teaching using classroom examples and survey and interview data.

Organization

The relationship between emotions and critical ELT is a new area of exploration for me. Therefore, I was unsure how the book would evolve until I was well into it; even then, it seemed to be changing as I wrote, leading me in unexpected directions. The final shape of the book is discussed next.

Theories

Considering Emotions in Critical English Language Teaching: Theories and Praxis is organized into two parts: Theories and Praxis. The Theories section includes three chapters. The first chapter offers a rationale for considering emotions and a short discussion of emotions in traditional and critical ELT, as a contrast to the way I handle them in the book.

The bulk of Chapter 1, however, is devoted to what I call my social/emotional history. Using Sara Ahmed's concept of how we "feel our way" throughout our lives, attaching ourselves to different people, ideas, and places, I explore how my interest in critical teaching developed from childhood until now. Beginning with the influence of the 1963 civil rights March on Washington, I trace how political events shaped my thinking and feeling, including the anti-war movement in which I participated as a high school student and battles over literacy testing in the City University of New York where I've taught since 1985. Throughout this history, I highlight the emotions that guided me and sometimes stood in my way, but always taught me how to connect my passion and reason as I made my way personally and professionally.

Chapter 2 summarizes the research on emotions in English language teaching, beginning with cognitive approaches. Next I examine sociocultural approaches to emotions in the teacher education ELT literature. Then I discuss multidisciplinary approaches to research on emotion words and mind/body connections. Finally, I bring in critical applied linguists whose work includes emotions though not as extensively as I do in this book.

Chapter 3 takes up the work of those who examine emotions critically, beginning with contributors to the affective turn in critical theory from fields as varied as sociology, geography, political theory, and anthropology. Here I explore how affect and emotions are theorized, including relationships between them. This section looks at feminist theorists' work on emotions. Also included in this chapter are examples of research on critical teaching in which affect and emotions were taken into account. This is a prelude to the examples I offer in the rest of the book.

Praxis

The Praxis section of the book opens with Chapter 4, an exploration of Sara Ahmed's notion of sticky objects; that is, objects to which emotions adhere. Using data about teachers' and students' reactions to two sticky objects that figure prominently in English language teaching classes—dictionaries and cellphones—I examine differences in their reactions to these objects and implications of these differences for critical teaching.

Chapter 5 takes up affect in Deleuzian terms, revisiting lessons on military recruitment I have written about previously. In this chapter I reinterpret the same lessons through the lenses of "becoming," a momentary suspension of the teacher/student binary, and a pedagogy of friendship. I also revisit an out-of-class experience in which I become a counter recruiter spontaneously, another example of becoming that transcended traditional identities.

Chapter 6 describes how I applied Claire Kramsch's notions about embodied selves in foreign language acquisition to two contexts: an undergraduate language acquisition course and an ESL reading class. In both I asked students to come up with metaphors for second language acquisition (SLA), using Kramsch's prompts, as a way to discover how embodied emotions come into play. The chapter suggests ways that emotions might be introduced to engage SLA students in building and interrogating theory, rather than simply absorbing what is already in place.

Chapter 7 takes up the emotional labor teachers perform that is for the most part unacknowledged and under-researched. Based on interviews, this chapter outlines various types of teachers' emotion work: emotion management, embodied work, and explicitly teaching emotions.

Chapter 8, the concluding chapter, offers suggestions for future work on emotions in critical ELT, tying up loose ends, and leaving some untied.

ACKNOWLEDGMENTS

Carrying out this project required the participation and support of many people. First, is the extraordinary Naomi Silverman who was also the editor of my 2001 book, *Critical English for Academic Purposes: Theory, Politics, and Practice*. In spring 2009 I met with Naomi to discuss a few possible ideas for a new book. She liked all of the ideas and encouraged me to choose one and write a prospectus. Rather than going with a familiar topic, such as critical EAP, I chose the one I felt least comfortable taking on, emotions and critical teaching, thinking it was time to shake myself up. Naomi, in her usual gracious and focused way, ushered the proposal through, getting me a contract in short order and sending me on my way.

A very special note of gratitude goes to Christian Chun, Martha Lewis, Howard Lewis, and Stephanie Vandrick, who read all or some of the chapters and gave me extraordinarily valuable feedback. While Christian and Stephanie are "in the field" and therefore offered the important perspective of my target audience, Martha and Howard were my lay audience yet their comments were equally useful.

On a more personal level, the time I spent with Christian, Stephanie, and Suhanthie Motha at the International Society of Language Studies in Aruba in June 2011 was particularly gratifying because I had the chance to talk over my ideas informally, you know, around the hotel pool. My overnight in July 2011 at the Lewis's charming cottage in upstate New York offered much-needed R and R during the last weeks of manuscript preparation.

Without the participation and responses of many English language teachers, I could not have written chapters 4 and 7. Their comments were invaluable in applying theories about emotions to actual classroom practice. So thanks to the following for filling out the surveys on cellphones and dictionaries and/or being interviewed about their teaching: Chrisanthi Anastopoulou; David Bridston; Gay

Brookes; Lisa Canino-Dymbort; Martha Clark Cummings; Effie Cochran; Christian Chun; Elaine Caputo-Ferrara; Len Fox; Elisabeth Gareis; Howard Kleinman; Maria Jerskey; Keming Liu; Barbara Murphy; Lenka Rohls; Abeer Samhoury; Rachel Sanchez; Kristina Scragg; Christopher Slattery; and Stephanie Vandrick. I also thank the teachers who preferred to remain anonymous.

The following students in my spring 2011 Language Acquisition class participated in the assignments described in Chapter 6 and I thank them for their thoughtful responses: Amal Aythh; Kristina DiBenedetto; Danny Duong; Nicole Figueroa; Ilya Geller; Amitai Glaser; Daniel Golat; Zeinab Imam; Alexis Kagans; Alba Kavaja; Jacquelyn Kratz; Haixin Li; Melissa Tinaphong; Christopher Wegenaar; and Colin Wu. Thanks, too, to the students who chose to remain anonymous.

In my wonderful neighborhood, Park Slope, Brooklyn, I'm surrounded by institutions that enhance my everyday life. Number one is the Park Slope Food Coop, the longest-running member-run food coop in the US. Without access to the excellent produce we get from local farmers, the job of writing this book would have been much harder. What would I have done without my lacinato kale? I'm not sure how orthodox it is to thank a food coop in book acknowledgments, but being a member is an honor and I deeply appreciate the work of the farmers, suppliers, coordinators, and member-shoppers who make it run so smoothly, against all odds.

I also acknowledge the local public institutions that fight for their lives in this neoliberal era of budget cuts and privatization: Brooklyn Academy of Music (BAM); Brooklyn Museum; Brooklyn Public Library; Brooklyn Botanical Gardens; and Prospect Park. These places sustain me and other Brooklynites almost daily and I will continue to contribute to them as they have to my well-being. The great independent films shown at BAM and the fabulous concerts in Prospect Park and Brooklyn Bridge Park kept me going throughout the time I wrote, as did the readings at the library and flora at the gardens.

The people in Park Slope, and other New York City hoods, who sweeten my life must also be acknowledged: Robert Attanasio; Harry Auerbach; Mimi Bluestone; Alison Brunell; Grace Cho; Marc Eskenazi; Ellen Fenton; Rochelle Goldstein; Ruth Herzlinger; Carolyn Kohli; Christine Mielenhausen; Herb Perr; Jane Quinn; Terry Quinn; Javier Santiago; Gary Shelton; and Carol Stein-Sapir.

I also want to acknowledge the City University of New York, and especially the College of Staten Island, my professional home since 1985. Like the other public institutions I cited, this one is under attack from those who oppose government spending and taxation of even the richest citizens. We fight constantly to sustain this university, a place where any high school graduate can attend college. It's worth the fight. To my colleagues in the English department who have supported and enhanced the ESL program, I thank you: Christanthi Anastopoulou; Alyson Bardsley; Bill Bernhardt; Kelly Bradbury; Robert Brandt; David Bridston; Lisa Canino-Dymbort; Ashley Dawson; Janet Dudley; Maryann Feola; Katie Goodland; Omar Hamad; Gail Hernandez; Peter Miller; Barbara Murphy; Jodi Pugliese; Mary Reda; Lenka Rohls; Abeer Samhoury; Rachel Sanchez; Sarah Schulman; and Christina Tortora.

For lightening-speed help with interlibrary loan requests I thank Dorothy Walsh. For keeping my computer humming, I thank Warrick Bell.

Finally, I thank my family, Joan, Amy, and Jane Benesch, my brother-in-law, Ray Gamache, and cousins Zee Jay and Jerry Greenspan and Deborah Sagner for their unflagging support throughout the writing process. And I thank my late father, Bill Benesch, physicist, birder, photographer, for having always encouraged my love of learning.

PART 1
Theories

1
INTRODUCTION, RATIONALE, AND MY SOCIAL/EMOTIONAL HISTORY

Introduction

Considering Emotions in Critical English Language Teaching: Theories and Praxis is a book I could not have written earlier in my career. Steeped in the politics of postsecondary English language teaching (ELT) in publicly-funded US universities, I was drawn to ways that critical theory helped explain identity and power relations in that context. I wasn't yet ready to examine the relationship between emotions and criticality in ELT.

Of course I had been aware of my own strong emotions related to ELT: dismay at how US colleges position immigrant students as linguistically and academically deficient; joy when students discussed assigned readings and their writing animatedly; discouragement when they seemed less engaged; worry on the days when high-stakes tests were administered; indignation when deserving students failed those literacy tests; pride on seeing some graduate.

As aware as I was of my own emotional states, I did not have ways of theorizing the relationship between emotions, classroom events, and sociopolitical issues. Because critical theory hadn't yet explicitly connected emotions and power, it was easy to overlook their place in institutional and classroom contexts. So, rather than examining the interrelatedness of emotions, education, and social factors, I acted on my strongest emotions. More specifically, my anger drove my writing about the failure of postsecondary institutions to welcome and accommodate diasporic students. At the start of my career, it fueled my critique of exclusionary testing and tracking policies that kept these students out of the academic mainstream (Benesch 1993).

Later, I indignantly explored how modernist beliefs about language and identity guided testing and tracking policies by constructing immigrant students as underprepared for college study (Benesch 2007a; 2009). An example is my critique of modernist concepts underlying the "discourses of partiality" (Benesch 2008, p. 294) circulating around the discussion of so-called generation 1.5 students. From my perspective the generation 1.5 trope constructs multicultural students as demographically, linguistically, and academically partial, thereby contributing to their marginalization, and I urged more complex understandings of their situations. My outrage also inspired me to argue for changes in how English language learners are not just positioned but also taught, proposing critical English for academic purposes (Benesch 1999; 2001).

Rationale

Whereas indignation propelled my writing in the past, I now want to examine a broad range of emotions, my own and others', from a social perspective.[1] This expanded research agenda entails considering ways that emotions shift and how they interconnect with power and bodies in classrooms, postsecondary institutions, and societies. Grounding my exploration in feminist and critical theories that link affect and criticality (Ahmed, 2004a, 2004b, 2010; Albrecht-Crane, 2005; Boler 1999; Massumi, 2002; Zemblyas 2005), I try to answer the following questions in this book:

- How have emotions and affect been theorized from critical perspectives in other fields?
- How might these theories of emotions be applied to research about critical English language teaching and learning?
- How might attention to emotions help to better understand and/or enhance critical English teaching and learning?

When beginning to answer these questions about emotions and critical teaching, the first book I read was Megan Boler's (1999) *Feeling Power: Emotions and Education*. That such a book existed, one linking emotions, power, and education, was a revelation. In it Boler discusses her frustration, when she was a student of philosophy, that emotions had been ignored, even in theories of subjectivity and epistemology that challenged positivism. She concluded that emotions' "absent-presence" (p. xv) was due to the long-standing tradition in philosophy and science of splitting truth/reason and subjectivity/emotions with emotions "positioned on the 'negative' side of the binary division" (p. xv). Women, she surmised, were also on the negative side, seen as driven irrationally by emotions.

So, Boler changed her scholarly pursuit from philosophy to history of consciousness, an interdisciplinary field, allowing her to investigate the causes of emotion's absence–presence. Studying a range of texts in philosophy, anthropology, psychology, and other disciplines, through the lenses of cultural studies, semiotics, and feminist theories, she focused on how knowledge is produced and transmitted discursively and commercially. Yet, Boler did not stop there. She brought her findings about the social construction of scholarly knowledge to her concern for social justice, aiming to investigate "how emotion shapes how we treat other people and informs our moral assumptions and judgments"(pp. xvi–xvii). Her driving force was pedagogical: to transform "violent practices of cruelty and injustice which are often rooted in unspoken 'emotional' investments" (p. xvii) through critical teaching.

Though Boler's questions about the social construction of knowledge differ from mine, focused on critical English language teaching, I appreciate her incisive mapping of the history of the exclusion of emotions from scholarly work. And I have been guided by her encouragement to "'recuperate' emotions from their shunned status, and reclaim them in new ways through embodied and ethical practices" (p. xxiv). I hope this book fulfills that call in even small ways.

While Boler's book was the first I read as I embarked on my search for how to examine emotions in critical ELT, Sara Ahmed's (2004a, 2004b, 2010) work has been the most influential on my thinking, particularly when it comes to theorizing emotions and affect. There are a few reasons for her strong influence. One is that she not only challenges the hierarchical placement of emotions as more primitive than reason but also the ranking of emotions themselves, with some being seen as higher or positive and others lower or negative. Ahmed's opposition to these rankings is significant in discussing emotions and ELT where certain emotions, such as anxiety, have traditionally been deemed harmful to language acquisition while others, such as enthusiasm, are considered helpful. In Chapter 2, I critique these rankings when discussing cognitive approaches to affect in SLA.

Related to Ahmed's (2004a) challenge to ranking emotions is her interest in power and emotions, seen in her study of "processes whereby 'being emotional' comes to be seen as a characteristic of some bodies and not others" (p. 4). To carry out this work, she replaces the conventional question of what emotions *are* with what emotions *do*. That is, she looks at "how emotions circulate between bodies examining how they 'stick' as well as move" (p. 4). This focus allows her to transcend arguments about differences between emotions and affect, so prominent in the work of affect theorists whose work is discussed in Chapter 3. Rather than taking sides in that polemic, she studies the "cultural politics" of emotions (p. 4). One key concept Ahmed proposes in this regard is "sticky objects," or sticky signs (p. 10); that is, objects, ideas, and words to which emotions adhere. Finding this concept not only approachable and tangible, but also researchable, I made it the focus of Chapter 4, the first chapter of the Praxis section.

Finally, alongside my appreciation of Ahmed's contributions as a theorist and someone offering concepts that are applicable to teaching contexts, is her background as the daughter of an immigrant father from Pakistan. This position leads her to explore the emotional complexities of immigrant life in the UK and their relationship to the politics of immigration, something she draws upon in her discussion of "happy" and "unhappy" immigrants (Ahmed 2010), discussed in chapters 3 and 7.

My preference for Ahmed's work has not led me, however, to exclude that of affect theorists, whose work is grounded in Spinoza's and Deleuze's. Instead, along with summarizing affect theorists' concepts, I devote Chapter 5 to an analysis of affect in my lessons about military recruitment on a US college campus, revisiting an earlier account of that pedagogy. Basing Chapter 5 on Albrecht-Crane and Stack's (2003) "pedagogy of affect" and Albrecht-Crane's proposal of "pedagogy of friendship," I look at how Deleuze's notions of "becoming" and "lines of flight" conceptualize those classroom moments when, even briefly, teachers and students abandon their proscribed identities and roles when experiencing and expressing fresh insights.

In the next two sections of this introductory chapter, I will briefly discuss the current treatment of emotions in ELT, both mainstream and critical literatures. This discussion shows that while attention to emotions is present in various ELT publications, emotions are either tangential, not taken up from a critical perspective, or not theorized. Though I go into greater depth about affect in the ELT literature in Chapter 2, where I summarize current research more thoroughly, my aim in the current chapter is to show that *Considering Emotions in Critical English Language Teaching: Theories and Praxis* fills a gap in the ELT literature, as part of my rationale.

The remainder of the chapter is an exploration of how my desire to link criticality and emotions developed from my personal and professional histories. My goal in including this narrative in the final section is to link the personal and political in order to "recuperate emotion not as an irrational bodily reaction but as an informed and political bodily response" (Gorton 2007, p. 343). The discussion of what I call my social/emotional history, then, is a prelude to examining theories and praxis in subsequent chapters where I lay out major assumptions related to emotions, criticality, bodies, and pedagogy more deeply.

Affect and Cognition in the Mainstream ELT Literature

Krashen's Affective Filter

This book is certainly not the first publication to call for attention to emotions in the field of English language teaching. In fact, emotions have been a feature of the work of many ELT specialists, though perhaps not as centrally as I'm calling for here, and not from a critical perspective. Possibly the best-known example, going back to the late 1970s and early 1980s, is Stephen Krashen's (1982) hypothesis that language acquisition is dependent on lowering what he called the "affective filter" (p. 9).

The affective filter was one of five hypotheses about second language acquisition Krashen offered, the others being the acquisition-learning distinction, the natural order hypothesis, the monitor hypothesis, and the input hypothesis. First proposed by Dulay and Burt in 1977 (as cited in Krashen 1982), the affective filter hypothesis claims that three "attitudinal factors" (p. 31) contribute to successful second language acquisition: high motivation; strong self-confidence; and low anxiety.

Krashen further hypothesized that those acquiring second languages vary in "strength or level of their Affective Filters" (p. 31). The variation was due to whether or not the above-mentioned attitudinal factors were optimal. Those with unfavorable attitudes were seen as having a "high or strong Affective Filter" while those with favorable attitudes were said to have "a lower or weaker filter" (p. 31).

As a nativist, or innatist, who subscribed to Chomskyan notions of language acquisition, including the language acquisition device (LAD), Krashen attempted to discover what conditions promoted linguistic input to the LAD. So, for example, he claimed that:

> [t]hose whose attitudes are not optimal for second language acquisition will not only tend to seek less input, but they will also have a high or strong Affective Filter – even if they understand the message, the input will not reach the part of the brain responsible for language acquisition, or the language acquisition device.
>
> (p. 31)

Because Krashen believed that "affective variables" impeded or facilitated "the delivery of input to the language acquisition device" (p. 32), he concluded that an important role for language teachers was to create a classroom climate that lowered students' anxiety, or affective filter, so that input could reach their LADs.

Though Krashen's hypotheses have been criticized for being difficult to test and overly mechanistic, his legacy persists, as seen in the cognitive literature discussed next in which emotions continue to be sorted into good and bad for language acquisition. In addition, one of the roles of language teachers, according to that literature, is still seen as reducing students' negative emotions so that learning may take place. In other words, like Krashen, more recent cognitive ELT theorists locate emotions within learners and do not look beyond them for more social explanations of the dynamics of emotions. However, as I'll discuss next, some do consider teachers' affect and its possible impact on students, an area not taken up in Krashen's affective filter hypothesis. This brief review is followed by a longer discussion of cognitive approaches to ELT in Chapter 2.

Cognitive Approaches to Affect in ELT

Jane Arnold's 1999 collection, *Affect in Language Learning*, offers cognitive and humanistic perspectives on the relationship between second/foreign language teaching and affect. According to Arnold, the chapters in the collection share the humanistic goal of "a desire to contribute to the growth of human potential" (p. xiii). In the first chapter, co-written by Arnold and H.D. Brown, affect is paired with cognition: "When both are used together, the learning can be constructed on a firmer foundation" (p. 1).

Emotions in language learning, according to Arnold and Brown, can be sorted into two types: those leading to successful language learning and those that stand in its way. Emotions associated with learning, such as motivation, are seen as positive;

those associated with impaired learning, such as anxiety, are deemed negative. The teacher's role, from this perspective, is to help students overcome negative emotions so that successful language learning may take place. They do this by first helping learners locate the source of their anger, frustration, anxiety, and so on. Teachers then encourage students to express those negative feelings "and then to move beyond them to acquire the new language at the same time as they also become proficient in the new culture" (p. 23).

Alongside the focus on students' emotions that bolster or block language learning there is interest in this literature in teachers' affectivity, a feature of what Arnold and Brown (1999) call "relational factors" (p. 18). Here the concern is with "intergroup behavior" in the classroom (p. 19), the smooth functioning of which relies on teacher empathy. To achieve greater empathy for their students, teachers must "move into closer contact with their own feelings" in order to "model empathic behavior in their dealings with students and to lead them to greater cross-cultural empathy" (p. 19). Thus the goals are not only enhanced language learning but also "the growth of emotional competence" (p. 24).

Having briefly acknowledged in this section that there is indeed an ELT literature taking affect into account, let me point out how my approach differs from the cognitive/humanistic one discussed by Arnold and Brown. First, emotions in this book will not be viewed as features of individuals' private psychologies. Rather, I theorize emotions in two other ways: 1) as socially constructed and embodied, in the feminist tradition; and 2) through the lens of affect theorists, grounded in the work of Giles Deleuze, who also sees affect as embodied as well as an area of free-floating possibility, unattached to social positioning or roles.

I realize that embracing both feminist notions of emotions and Deleuzian notions of affect could be seen as theoretically inconsistent. However, I find both constructs sufficiently powerful that I'm willing to sacrifice theoretical purity in the name of adopting both as useful lenses for critical ELT. In fact, in Chapter 5 where these two theoretical positions overlap, it is possible to see how they may be more complementary than inconsistent or contradictory.

In addition, I do not characterize emotions monolithically as either positive or negative. Instead, I consider them as shifting and interacting, in relationship to the social context in which they are felt and/or expressed. Nor do I associate particular emotions with successful or unsuccessful language learning because I don't posit a causal relationship between affect and language learning. Instead, I will describe how emotions shift and move, sticking to a variety of ideas, words, and objects, influencing teaching and learning. Finally, I will not be pairing emotions with cognition, but, rather, with criticality, a topic I turn to next.

Emotions and Criticality in the Critical ELT Literature

To establish a relationship between emotions and criticality, I first have to define what I mean by *critical* in teaching contexts. My preferred definition is from Luke

(2004) who describes critical engagement as " ... the out-of-body experience of watching oneself watch oneself as an object of power and naming oneself as such" (p. 28). This definition paints a clear picture of the process of critical analysis, or what Luke calls "self-othering": that is, "a sense of being beside oneself or outside oneself in another epistemological discourse, and political space than one typically would inhabit" (p. 26).

However, self-othering can be challenging, even daunting, because it requires stepping outside one's customary ways of thinking and feeling. Indeed, Luke acknowledges a possible emotional response to critical engagement in his description of the process. He explains that because critical thinking entails "some actual dissociation from one's available explanatory texts and discourses" it can lead to "discomfort" due to "making the familiar strange" (Luke 2004, pp. 26–27). Nonetheless, while acknowledging the discomfort critical analysis might cause, Luke and other critical ELT theorists do not consider emotions centrally nor theorize them systematically.

Though the critical ELT literature is surprisingly quiet when it comes to theorizing emotions, there are a few examples of attention to affectivity. One of the best-known and most compelling is the identity work of Bonny Norton. Her research on English language learning and use among immigrant women in Canada demonstrated that the psychological concept of motivation was inadequate for characterizing the complex relationship between learners, language, and society. Norton (2000) found that although the women she interviewed were "highly motivated, there were particular conditions under which [they] were most *uncomfortable* [emphasis added] and unlikely to speak" (p. 120). These conditions related to the learners' shifting identities (mother, wife, worker, working-class immigrant) and their varying reception as immigrants in Canada.

To capture the complexity of learners' identities, Norton replaced the psychological term *motivation* with the social term *investment*:

> A learner's motivation to speak is mediated by other investments that may conflict with the desire to speak – investments that are intimately connected to the ongoing production of learners' identities and their desires for the future.
>
> (p. 120)

It is interesting to note the affective terms Norton employs in discussing her research: uncomfortable, desire, intimately connected. She also mentions the participants' tendency to feel "*ashamed, inferior, and uninteresting* [emphasis added] because of their second language abilities" (p. 123). What adds strength and dimension to Norton's analysis is that she clearly links these feelings to power relations guiding the women's social interactions.

To further the connection between identity, language learning, power, and society, Norton offers the observation that learner anxiety is not innate or cognitive, but, rather, "socially constructed within and by the lived experiences of language learners" (ibid). This is a striking contrast to the understanding of emotions posited by Krashen's affective filter and the more recent contributions of cognitive ELT theorists.

Norton's work is an important precedent to considering emotions from a critical perspective. Her descriptions of the complex socially-constructed emotions displayed and expressed by the immigrant women in her study as well as Luke's allusion to the discomfort of self-othering point to the need for greater attention in critical ELT to the relationship between emotions and criticality.

Feeling My Way: My Social/Emotional History

> Where does this kind of critical questioning and attention to power relations come from? Is it innate? Does it come about by chance? Or, is it a unique product of prior family and community experiences?
>
> (Morgan, 2009, p. 87)

> ... emotions "matter" for politics; emotions show us how power shapes the very surfaces of bodies as well as worlds. So in a way, we do "feel our way".
>
> (Ahmed, 2004a, p. 12)

Brian Morgan poses intriguing questions about what leads individuals and groups to take critical stances toward the status quo. As I outline in this overview of my personal and professional histories, my own critical questioning started early, yet I attribute it not to innateness but rather to social conditions. The historical moment in which I grew up (the mid-1950s and the 1960s), the place where I was raised and attended school (Washington DC), and certain key events, all played a role in shaping my current interest in criticality and its relationship to emotions in critical teaching.

In this discussion of key events and some of the emotions that seemed, in retrospect, to co-exist with each other and the events, I will explore Sara Ahmed's (2004a) claim that "emotions 'matter' for politics" and that we "feel our way" (p. 12) as we live our lives, making personal, political, and professional choices. Though I borrow Ahmed's concept of feeling our way, I do not, in the discussion of my social/ emotional history, offer a theorized understanding of emotions, affect, or feeling. Theorizing these terms is the job of Chapter 3, where I move from the anecdotal approach of this chapter to a social and embodied understanding of emotions in critical theories.

I do show in my social/emotional history, however, how my emotions interacted with social events and were, therefore, neither private nor psychological. That is, in the remainder of this chapter I outline connections between the social world in which I lived and the predominant emotions I experienced at the time, at least as I recall them from my current perspective. Yet, this is not a tracing of cause and effect relationships, but instead an attempt to consider how my social and affective lives coincided, how emotions guided me as I felt my way through the exhilarating and tumultuous 1960s and early 1970s in Washington DC, college life in the mid

1970s, and New York City in the late 1970s to the present day. I divide this history into three periods: Social unrest as critical training ground; Leaving home/seeking home; Contradictions of CUNY (City University of New York): pull and push.

Social Unrest as Critical Training Ground

I grew up in Washington DC in the 1960s, a time of great social upheaval and change in the United States and around the world. In 1963, when I was eight years old, the March on Washington, led by Reverend Martin Luther King, took place just a few miles from where my family lived. I pleaded with my parents to take me with them, sensing, even at that young age, that this event was not to be missed. Concerned that I was too young and unsure of what would transpire that day, they urged me to watch the historical proceedings on television. I witnessed an integrated group of 250,000 people congregating peacefully for civil rights, with the US Capitol building, the Washington monument, and the Lincoln Memorial as backdrops.

That thrilling and inspiring event was followed by a series of terrifying murders of US leaders between 1963 and 1968: the assassinations of President John Kennedy, Dr. King, and Robert Kennedy. Parents and teachers seemed bewildered by the violence of these public acts and ill-equipped to mediate them. On the days President Kennedy and Dr. King were murdered, we were simply let out of school with no explanation of why, left to our own devices and rumors, trying to make sense of what had happened.[2] School administrators seemed afraid of our possibly strong reactions, maybe too busy processing their own.

The lack of adult guidance in coming to terms with the violence around us, though destabilizing, encouraged young people to organize ourselves. Adult leaders were being murdered, but youth leaders emerged, urging us to become involved in shaping our history. Coming of age in the 1960s meant challenging what had come before, as it had for prior generations. But in our case, we were guided by discourses of protest and dissent; we rejected adult culture, subscribing to the rhetoric of the *counter culture* and the *generation gap*. I embraced the trappings passionately: bell bottoms, love beads, the Doors, black-light posters.

Yet, my connection to events was deeper than the accessories and paraphernalia, especially when it came to the anti-war movement; that is, opposition to the US military engagement in Vietnam. Swept up in the immediacy and urgency of politics in DC in 1968, I supported Eugene McCarthy, who ran for US president on an anti-war platform. I was 14 years old, working in his campaign office and distributing literature.

My involvement in the anti-war movement increased after the killing of four unarmed college students at Kent State University by members of the Ohio National Guard on Monday, May 4, 1970. This flashpoint mobilized an increasing number of students in my high school, leading to almost daily bomb scares and heated debates with our teachers and parents. We participated in anti-war demonstrations regularly, traveling by city bus to the White House or Washington Monument to march with hand-made signs demanding an end to the war. These were scary and confusing times, but also exhilarating. To be a teenager protesting against the US government's bombing in Southeast Asia alongside people who had traveled to DC from all over the country was to feel part of something larger and more important than the mundane obligations of school: attendance, tests, grades, homework.

Leaving Home/Seeking Home

It seems incredible that anyone graduated from high school in DC in 1972, given the charged racial and political climates, and compelling extracurricular activities, but I did and entered college in St. Louis that fall. There I met peers from across the US. However, I found myself gravitating toward international students, maybe out of a sense of alienation from the war and my tumultuous teenage life. I attended events at the International House and even led some ESL conversation classes as a sophomore.

During my junior year, I studied at the University of Strasbourg, France, where I spent one day a week observing and teaching EFL in a middle school. My only training for that work was a foreign-language-teaching methods course, from an audio-lingual perspective, I had taken the previous year at my US university. The highlight was chaperoning a group of pre-teens on the annual trip to London, along with the school's English teachers.

After graduating from college in 1976, I spent a few months in Paris where I was introduced to the Silent Way, a then-popular language teaching method in private French companies offering government-mandated adult education to their employees. The materials and techniques were compelling because they provided what seemed at the time to be a coherent and sensible system for representing a language. After the chaos of high school and the exciting but disorienting college years, I was ready to embrace that system wholeheartedly and devotedly: color-coded sound and word charts, Cuisenaire rods, pointers, and the philosophy of subordinating teaching to learning (Gattegno 1963).

I accepted the premise that the materials, though on the surface rigid and uncompromising, freed the teacher to focus on students' learning rather than on the language. Silencing the teacher so she could listen to the students was also an appealing countercultural concept even if what the students uttered was largely directed by the silent teacher, especially at the early stages.

After taking a Silent Way workshop in Paris, I returned to DC where I got a job by marketing myself as a teacher of this method. About once a month I traveled to New York City to study with Caleb Gattegno, the developer of the Silent Way, eager to learn as much as I could and be part of that world. His school, Educational Solutions, was a thrilling place to be at that time in my life. On the fourteenth floor of 80 Fifth Avenue, staff members from around the world were manufacturing materials and packaging them for shipment, welcoming guests and students, and leading workshops in various languages. A year after beginning my studies with Gattegno, he hired me to work at Educational Solutions. So I moved to New York

City in 1979 and joined the staff, becoming a Silent Way teacher of French and ESL at the school/company.

My time at Educational Solutions was dedicated to perfecting my Silent Way teaching techniques and absorbing the philosophy, including taking and giving weekend workshops. The main tenets of the philosophy I took to heart were: if students show up to class, assume they are ready to learn; attend to the differences between teaching and learning; students work on the language while the teacher works on students' awareness. These lessons have stayed with me and inform my teaching to this day. Though they are not explicitly critical, the subordination of teaching to learning is a precept that implicitly upends traditional power relations, putting students' awareness first and calling on the teacher to quiet herself so she can attend to her students' learning.[3]

While working at Educational Solutions, I got my MA in TESOL from New York University, going to school at night. However, I was such an ardent devotee of the Silent Way that it was hard for me to absorb what was being taught in my graduate courses. My dismissal of anything but Gattegno's work prevented me from considering other ideas. It may also be that the anti-intellectual climate in the MA TESOL program in those days offered few, if any, compelling alternatives. There was no theory, just practice.

It was only when I entered the PhD program in English Education and was introduced to the field of composition that I began to consider others' ideas as relevant and intellectually-engaging. The approach at the time, 1982–85, was cognitive, with a focus on process writing. I studied the work of Douglas Barnes, Ann Berthoff, James Britton, Ken Bruffee, William Coles, Peter Elbow, Nancy Martin, Peter Medway, James Moffett, and others in the field of composition, including my engaging professors, Lil Brannon, John Mayher, Gordon Pradl, and Geoffrey Summerfield. James Britton and Nancy Martin also offered workshops during the summer, a great opportunity to learn directly from them.

Early in my doctoral studies I also read Mark Clarke's (1982) compelling article, "On Bandwagons, Tyranny, and Common Sense", one that helped me put my devotion to the Silent Way in perspective. The article begins with a denunciation of bandwagons as being not only trendy, but also extremist, authoritarian, all-encompassing, dramatic, and dependent on a bag of tricks. These attributes could certainly be applied to the Silent Way and I had been swept up in the drama as a true believer. Clarke also points to a culture of condescension toward those who do not climb on to the bandwagon, something I had experienced as a staff member at Educational Solutions.

However, the article takes a surprising and touching turn that helped me to forgive myself for my ardor and condescension when working for Gattegno. In a bold and humble move, Clarke admits that he himself had climbed onto a bandwagon at the start of this career, becoming a devotee of audio-lingualism. To make sense of this stage of his professional life, he explains that "[o]ne must begin somewhere" (p. 446). He also outlines the reasons why a young and inexperienced scholar might become so attached to a method or school of thought: they offer confidence, company ("the security that we are working side-by-side with others" p. 447), and techniques. The reassurance from Mark Clarke that he, and probably others, had abandoned themselves wholeheartedly to a method when first starting out, as I had with the Silent Way, allowed me to put my zealotry in context and even to embrace aspects of the philosophy that stayed with me.[4]

Paulo Freire's (1970) *Pedagogy of the Oppressed*, assigned for one of my PhD courses, made a huge impression in terms of educational philosophy, but I did not see its direct application to my teaching. The students in the composition courses I taught at NYU as part of my graduate assistantship were hardly oppressed. They were privileged students living in dormitories, unencumbered by jobs or family responsibilities.

Contradictions of CUNY: Pull and Push

In 1985, I was hired as an assistant professor at the College of Staten Island (CSI), one of 17 colleges of the City University of New York (CUNY), the largest urban publicly-funded university in the US. I was thrilled to have a tenure-track job and excited to be part of a public educational system again as I had been in high school. CUNY's open admissions policy (to admit all New York City high school graduates), appealed to my sense of social justice and I couldn't wait to join the English department and start teaching ESL courses to immigrant students. Becoming a CUNY faculty member promised to integrate various parts of my history: civil rights, inter-cultural communication, TESOL, and composition theory.

However, my idealism was tested as I settled into the new job. It was immediately obvious that CUNY's open admissions policy was more of a battleground than the fulfillment of a civil rights dream. The promise and pull of open admissions was countered by the push of literacy tests, pre-requisites, and partial or no credit for ESL. Powerful gates had been erected, raising serious doubts about CUNY's democratic mission.

The reading and writing, so-called proficiency, tests were given to entering students. Scores on these literacy tests, as well as the math proficiency test, were used to determine placement. Those achieving a passing score went directly to credit-bearing English, math, and other general education classes. Those receiving lower scores were placed in ESL or remedial classes for which some credit was offered at that time. The writing test was an essay graded by two readers while the reading test was multiple choice. Both were timed.

Not only were the literacy tests used to exclude students from credit-bearing courses; in addition, the required first-year composition course was a pre-requisite for many other courses in the college. Entering students therefore had to navigate a dizzying maze of tests, retests, pre-college courses, and pre-requisites, a discouraging set of conditions they had not been alerted to, for the most part, before arriving to register. Nor were their counterparts at private colleges subject to such barriers.

I was being groomed to assume the position of ESL coordinator in the English department and thereby a tacit supporter of CUNY's testing and tracking policies. As an administrator, I would have to enforce current policies by explaining to students that they could not take credit-bearing courses until passing the reading and writing tests. These barriers felt akin to the literacy tests imposed on black voters in the southern US prior to the civil rights movement, and therefore unjust, even possibly criminal.[5] In 1960s' parlance, as ESL coordinator, I would be part of the problem, unless I found a way to contribute to the solution.

Adding to my discomfort, I was a young assistant professor in a department that had not hired any new faculty in ten years. Therefore, I was, at the outset, socially adrift in the institution. Factions had formed long before and, to add to my outsider stance, the college was a commuter school far from where many of the faculty lived. So there was no built-in social life on campus, not even a room for faculty to gather. Students departed campus right after their classes were over to get to work and attend to family responsibilities. To make social life even more challenging, the college was housed on two campuses so my department had two separate locations, a few miles apart.

Fortunately, as a complex institution of contradictions, CUNY was not simply a site of banal admissions restrictions. It also contained a wonderfully diverse student population, intelligent and politically aware faculty, a faculty union, and the academic freedom to construct engaging curricula. To combat my isolation, I sought programs and groups that might offer solidarity and alternatives to the exclusion of ESL students from mainstream curricula. One such program was the Freshman Workshop Program (FWP) which offered blocks of three courses to English language learners and native speakers of English: reading, writing, and either business, social science, humanities, or science/technology. I was invited to join the FWP during my first semester at CSI and continued teaching in it many semesters thereafter (Benesch 1988, 1992).

The FWP provided students and faculty opportunities for connection, long before the notion of learning communities had been institutionalized. By enrolling in three linked courses, students could form bonds that would have been difficult to forge when taking several unconnected courses, each with a different group of peers. Faculty, too, could form relationships within and outside their departments, due to the collaborative structure of the program. For example, during my first few semesters at CSI, I taught an ESL writing course linked to a reading course taught by a colleague in my department and a social science class taught by a psychologist, Ivan Smodlaka. Ivan and I mentored each other. He offered moral support during the difficult first year, advising me about how to navigate the complexities of CSI and CUNY. I, a freshly-minted PhD, conveyed to him what I had just learned in graduate school about composition and pedagogy.

To address equity issues, I found support in the CUNY ESL Council, a forum established in 1971 by ESL specialists from across CUNY to work on curricular and policy issues. Other coordinators and teachers were equally concerned about the use of the reading and writing tests to exclude English language learners from mainstream, credit-bearing courses and sought ways to minimize their impact. We strategized together and met with administrators in the CUNY central office and expressed our concerns. One change we achieved was to have the amount of time increased on the reading test. However, literacy testing continues to this day and in some ways exclusion has deepened and broadened, with more pre-requisites and literacy tests that present even greater challenges to English language learners.

By the end of my first year at CSI, I was gratified to be involved with CSI colleagues in an intellectually stimulating program that encouraged students to interrogate academic material. At the university level, my CUNY ESL Council colleagues and I were addressing equity issues on an ongoing basis: testing, placement and credit for ESL courses. However, concerned that the wheels of change were hardly moving, I turned to the work of Paulo Freire (1970). His writing confirmed that change could only be made by analyzing power relations within the university and by organizing teachers and students. In Freire's terms, we faced a *limit-situation*; that is, an obstacle restricting freedom to pursue one's goals. To avoid hopelessly succumbing to the *limit-situations* created by literacy tests, pre-requisites, and lack of credit for ESL courses, we had to involve ourselves in *limit-acts*, attempts to defeat the obstacles. Yet, we were unsure of the outcome; we were engaged in *untested feasibility* (Freire 1970, p. 85).

By the time I assumed the ESL coordinator position, the state legislature had begun ordering English departments across New York State to remove existing credit from ESL courses on the grounds that the courses were, from their point of view, remedial. Though my colleagues and I argued that ESL was not remedial and presented the TESOL Member Resolution on Granting Credit for ESL in Institutions of Higher Education (www.tesol.org/s_tesol/sec_document.asp?CID=87&DID=231) as testimony to the state accreditation board, we were unsuccessful in persuading them to distinguish ESL and remediation. However, at CSI we did manage to achieve a compromise by reducing credits from three per course to three, two, and one respectively for the three levels of reading and writing. Nonetheless, a few years later, not content with that reduction, the state ordered the removal of all remaining credit for ESL courses.

Once all credits had been taken away from the three reading and writing ESL courses, I reluctantly accepted the fact that the highly charged political climate in New York State, including the tenuous relationship between the state legislature and CUNY, would make it impossible to retain or restore credit for ESL courses. However, rather than giving up entirely on that goal, I began to cast about for other ways to challenge the *limit-situation*. The *limit-act* I eventually settled on, with encouragement and support from colleagues, was to propose the addition of two ESL courses at a higher level than the existing ESL offerings. These two courses would compose a two-semester sequence of first-year composition already required of all students. In other words, we were asking for two sheltered ESL first-year composition courses for full credit, hoping that the college, CUNY, and the state would accept this initiative. Fortunately, the proposal went through; that addition to our ESL offerings, grounded in real politics, raised my spirits.

Yet, the battle to retain any remnants of open admissions continues. It is a constant source of tension, rage, defeat, and hope for those who subscribe to the mission. How those and other emotions circulate in English language classrooms and in the institutions where English is taught in immigrant-receiving countries is a focus of the rest of the book.

Toward Critical/Emotional Teaching

Reflecting on and writing my social/emotional history, a few themes emerged that relate to Ahmed's (2004a) assertion that I was "feeling my way" while engaging socially and politically. First is the theme of organizing for social change, a precept so dramatically demonstrated by the 1963 March on Washington I viewed on television as a child and learned about through the excitement of my parents and their friends who were present. The significance of political participation with like-minded citizens was also deeply felt during the protests in Washington against the US bombing of Southeast Asia during my teenage years. Fueling these events were the discourses of dissent and protest which themselves were propelled by hope, fury, and impatience.

The discourses of dissent and protest penetrated the walls of my secondary school, leading to curricular changes. For example, African American students demanded literature that reflected their experience, opposing the steady diet of dead white authors. Administrators and teachers responded by adding such texts as Claude Brown's (1965) *Manchild in the Promised Land*, John Howard Griffin's (1961) *Black Like Me*, and Ann Moody's (1968) *Coming of Age in Mississippi*, ones I read in my high school English courses.

One of the most compelling texts I studied at that time was Langston Hughes's (1951) poem, "Harlem," which spoke of the emotional and political costs of exclusion. The first line asks, "What happens to a dream deferred?" The famous second and third lines ask, "Does it dry up like a raisin in the sun?" and the last line, "Or does it explode?" These lines evoke a range of feelings in me from that era. Would the excluded continue to fight back until they destroyed the institutions that barred their entrance or would they give up in defeat, too discouraged to continue the fight for inclusion? What was my relationship to the struggle of blacks for equal rights in Washington and across the country?

My friends and I, liberal Jews, naïvely hoped that our black peers would welcome our support in their struggle and were narcissistically wounded when our overtures were rebuffed. This was their fight and they resented our attempts to join in, particularly because of the advantages we had had. Heated discussions were frequent in classrooms where African American literature had been assigned. Our teachers, unprepared to mediate, either threw up their hands or walked out of the classroom when arguments erupted, unsure of how to contend with the emotional content of the explosive books they had assigned and asked us to write about.

Perhaps because black and white students in my high school were unable to find common ground, the dream deferred is a message that has remained with me. The emotional cost of exclusion is a powerful theme, one I brought to my work at CUNY, hoping to confront it through my teaching and administration. My students are clearly demoralized and confused by the double message of open admissions and closed gates. As I have felt my way in the institution, I have concluded that part of my job is to explore the contradictions of CUNY with them so that they might understand that their exclusion is political, not due to their personal failure or inadequacy. We study the continued erosion of the public sector and its effects on urban life, including a degraded public transportation system that often fails to deliver students to the college on time, forcing them to leave home increasingly early, cutting into their sleeping hours, so precious for those who work and attend school. Connecting budget cuts to a diminished quality of life is a way for students to understand that their frustration and other feelings are both legitimate and tied to larger social issues.

At the same time, I acknowledge the pain students have experienced from repeated literacy testing and pre-requisites that prevent them from enrolling in mainstream, credit-bearing courses. Yet, due to my experience as a white high school student in Washington DC, I am mindful of the pitfalls of white liberalism, with its possibly patronizing stance toward those who have had fewer privileges. So I try to balance my awareness of white middle-class privilege with my desire for social justice in critical teaching.[6]

Dealing with the contradictions of CUNY, the draw of open admissions and the rebuff of exclusion from credit-bearing courses, for more than two decades has led me to seek nuanced ways of operating at various levels of the institution. In my early years I viewed the politics in a binary way: faculty vs. administration; inclusion vs. exclusion; student-friendly vs. student-hostile. However, I began to realize, as I felt my way, that the complexities called for a more subtle approach, requiring attention to the political climate and adjusted expectations grounded in real politics. I have learned to choose my battles carefully and to work pragmatically while not being resigned to the status quo. This more calibrated way of working requires navigating various emotions and, rather than demanding political purity, maintaining hope when goals are not achieved or even when gains are reversed.

Pedagogically speaking, I have begun to consider emotions more centrally, in the context of critical teaching, trying to bring together the politics of public education, language, testing, and my own and students' emotions. For example, in the past, when asking students about their experience taking the CUNY assessment tests, I would pose questions such as: What did you find most difficult about the tests? Now, I frame the question in a way that centralizes their emotional experience as an entree to larger issues: How did you feel while you were taking them? How did you feel when you received your scores? The range of feelings students express (anger, fear, nervousness, disappointment, confusion) are the platform from which we discuss why the tests exist and how to avoid being defeated by instruments of exclusion in all areas of their lives. I discuss this pedagogy further in Chapter 7 on teachers' emotion work.

This exploration of events that shaped my current interest in emotions in critical teaching is a prelude to the rest of the book in which I review relevant literatures and offer examples of emotions in critical praxis.

2

EMOTIONS IN ENGLISH LANGUAGE TEACHING

Related Literatures

This chapter explores how emotions have been taken up in various ELT literatures. The rationales and theoretical assumptions driving these literatures will be examined along with their differing definitions of affect and emotion. My goal in summarizing the research on emotions in ELT is to outline the contributions already made and those that have yet to be made, as groundwork for the next chapters in which critical theory underlies the conceptualization of emotions.

In the first section of this chapter, I discuss contributions to the ELT literature in which emotions are examined from a cognitive perspective, expanding on my brief description in Chapter 1. The next section focuses on sociocultural approaches to emotions in the teacher education ELT literature. In the subsequent section, I discuss the multidisciplinary approach taken by Aneta Pavlenko in her research on multilinguals' use of emotion words. Then I take up Kramsch's (2009) *The Multilingual Subject*, an examination of mind/body connections in foreign language learning. Though Kramsch does not address ELT, her research on language learning memoirs and students' metaphors for foreign and heritage language learning sheds important light on connections between their intellectual and emotional lives. Finally, I bring in critical applied linguistics where some work has been done to include emotions, though they have not been theorized to the extent that they might.[1]

The chapter concludes with an examination of differences between how I examine emotions in this book and the ways in which each of the literatures discussed in this chapter takes up emotions/affect.

Cognitive Approaches to Emotions in the ELT Literature

Cognitive approaches to emotions in ELT examine the partnership between emotions and cognition, to discover how emotions support or undermine language learning.

In this literature, emotions are theorized as individual learners' internal states that are either negatively or positively correlated with language learning. Some authors in this tradition locate emotions in the mind (Arnold 1999; Stevick 1999) while for others they originate in the brain (Schumann 1999). Still others discuss emotions as psychological states without referring to them as located in the mind or body (Ehrmann 1999; Horowitz 2001). Yet, despite these differences, all share what Ahmed (2004a) calls the "presumption of interiority"; that is, the assumption that "I have feelings and they are mine" (p. 8). In her review of various approaches to emotions, Ahmed calls this an "inside-out model" (p. 9) because emotions are assumed to originate inside individuals' minds or bodies and expressed or revealed externally.

Jane Arnold's 1999 collection, *Affect in Language Learning* is the key text I will discuss in this section. It includes several names long associated with cognition in ELT, including John Schumann, Rebecca Oxford, and Zoltan Dornyei. According to Arnold and H. Douglas Brown, co-authors of the first chapter in the collection, there are two reasons for attending to emotions in ELT. The first is "more effective language learning" (Arnold and Brown 1999, p. 2); the second, which they call the "expanded mandate," is to "educate learners to live more satisfying lives and to be responsible members of society" (p. 3).

Alongside the goal of improving language teaching is the assumption that emotions can be sorted into two categories when it comes to language learning: negative and positive. Negative emotions, such as anxiety and anger, are seen as impediments to language learning while positive emotions, such as self-esteem and motivation, are viewed as facilitators. This binary view of emotions as either good or bad for second language acquisition, though not grounded in nativism, is closely tied to assumptions driving Krashen's affective filter hypothesis, discussed in Chapter 1.

The second goal, the "expanded mandate," is based on the authors' support for Daniel Goleman's widely-discussed emotional literacy proposition which claims that many current social problems can be attributed to "emotional illiteracy" (p. 3); that is, "misusing or denying whatever falls within the realm of the emotions or non-rational" (p. 3). According to Goleman (2005), schools should intervene when children exhibit "deficits in emotional and social skills that undergird problems such as aggression or depression" (p. 262). In other words, in Goleman's formulation, aggression and depression do not reside in unfavorable or desperate social conditions, but rather in childrens' lack of emotional literacy. If only children would gain emotional intelligence, their negative feelings would vanish.

In the emotional literacy paradigm, schooling in emotional intelligence pays off in three ways: children learn to manage their negative emotions, they perform better in school, and the society benefits because of a reduction in aggressive behavior.[2] In ELT contexts, according to Arnold and Brown (1999), if teachers cultivated their own emotional literacy, they might then be able to help their students become emotionally literate which in turn would lead to both increased learning and more fulfilling lives.

An essential question in examining the literature on emotions, one I will raise throughout the book, is how the author(s) define (or theorize) emotions and affect. Equally important is to consider how the authors view the relationship between them. Arnold and Brown stake out the terrain in the following way: "In the present context, affect will be considered broadly as aspects of emotion, feeling, mood, or attitude which condition behavior" (p. 1).

There are two things to note in this formulation. One is that affect and emotion are not clearly differentiated, a stance taken by other, but not all, authors that I'll be discussing. The other is that affect/emotion seems to be considered as a precedent to behavior; that is, you experience an emotion internally and then you act on it, an example of Ahmed's "inside-out" model. Arnold and Brown may, in fact, have a more reciprocal understanding of the relationship between emotion and action, but the words they chose to explain it give the impression that they view affect as cause and action as effect. The physical experience of emotions and affect are not taken up. Cognitive theorists of emotions in ELT do not consider the body as part of the study of affect (though as I discuss later, Schumann takes the brain into account).

While overlooking the relationship between emotions and bodies, Arnold and Brown focus on the mind as the origin of affect, seeing "emotion and cognition as partners in the mind" (p. 1). From this perspective "emotions are a part of reason" (p.1) and, therefore, when affect and cognition are "used together, the learning process can be constructed on a firmer foundation" (p. 1). One might expect, given these cognitive assumptions, that the authors would be concerned exclusively with individual factors, such as anxiety, inhibition, extroversion/introversion, self-esteem, motivation, and learner styles, all of which they do indeed discuss. However, in addition, Arnold and Brown bring in three "relational factors" (p. 18): empathy, classroom transactions, and cross-cultural processes. Nonetheless, while claiming that the addition of these "relational factors" contributes to a "social focus" (p. 18), the authors' concern is individual learners in their interaction with others. Their approach to the social does not include an engagement with students' race, gender, class, and other identity issues involving power relations. Instead, the social in their cognitive/affective approach is restricted to one-to-one interactions between individual learners and their interlocuteurs, seen as a "transactional process ... intimately connected with the learner's emotional being" (p. 18).

Regarding one category of "relational factors," cross-cultural factors, the authors claim that when learning a second language, learners face "particular emotional difficulties produced by the confrontation between two cultures" (p. 21). Though this construction appears initially as social, in my view it is cognitive because it locates emotional experience within individual learners' minds, along with essentializing cultures as static and potentially adversarial. This individual/psychological perspective is driven home by the authors' description of the central role teachers are supposed to play when it comes to students' emotional responses to cultural dissonance: mediating possible cultural clashes.

To help students deal with "affective problems encountered in the process of adapting to the new culture and language" (p. 23), the authors recommend certain classroom activities, such as role playing and journal writing. The aim of the classroom assignments is to help learners locate the source of their anger, frustration, or anxiety, to express their feelings, "and *then to move beyond them* [emphasis added] to acquire the new language at the same time as they also become proficient in the new culture" (p. 23). In this formulation, as in Goleman's, so-called negative emotions are best acknowledged and then overcome to remove any impediments to linguistic and cultural proficiency, a formulation I question throughout this book.

The notion that an individual learner's "negative" emotions impede language learning and that they should therefore be transcended, with the support of teachers, also appears in Rebecca Oxford's (1999) chapter in the same collection. Though Oxford does not explicitly theorize emotions, her cognitive framework can be inferred. The unstated assumption is that emotions are internal states of individuals' minds; neither affect nor bodily feeling is mentioned in this chapter. Anxiety is the emotion Oxford explores, and more specifically, "language anxiety", defined as "anxiety linked directly to performing in the target language … not just a general performance anxiety" (p. 59).

According to Oxford, language anxiety is a highly influential factor in language learning. It may either be a "passing state" or "a trait" in cases when "repeated occurrences cause students to associate anxiety with language performance" (p. 60). While speculating that there might be occasions on which anxiety is positive or helpful, Oxford generally supports research findings pointing to "a negative relationship between anxiety and performance" (p. 60). Oxford ends her chapter with suggestions for teachers to help students reduce anxiety. These include boosting self-esteem, reducing competition, being clear about classroom goals, and encouraging moderate risk-taking.

Schumann (1999), too, distinguishes negative and positive emotions related to language learning, though his model is neurobiological, with its focus on the brain as the site of language acquisition and learning as the interaction between the nervous system and the environment. According to this model: "The brain evaluates the stimuli it receives via the senses from the language learning situation …, and this appraisal leads to an emotional response" (Schumann 1999, p. 28). Schumann claims that appraisals leading to emotional responses are along the following dimensions of experience: novelty and familiarity; pleasantness; goal or need significance; coping potential; and self and social image. Yet, he does not associate any particular dimension with either positive or negative appraisal. Instead, Schumann believes that second language learners could positively or negatively appraise any one of them due to the uniqueness of each brain. He also claims that "positive appraisals along any of the five dimensions promote SLA" (p. 37).

To illustrate how positive or negative appraisals along these dimensions might work, Schumann offers the example of Eva Hoffman's (1989) language learning experience described in her memoir, *Lost in Translation*. According to Schumann's analysis, after immigrating to Canada, Hoffman reacted very negatively to Canadian people and culture. Thus, on the dimension of pleasantness, her appraisal was negative. On the other hand, "her positive appraisals were dominant along the goal and self and social image dimensions" (p. 36). So, though Hoffman experienced events in Canada as unpleasant, she was able to succeed in learning English because these events correlated positively with eventually fulfilling her long-term goals.

Applying his hypotheses regarding appraisals and emotional responses to language teaching, Schumann concludes that, given each language learner's and language teacher's unique appraisal system, teachers should "negotiate their appraisals of the language learning situation with those of the students" (p. 38) in order to maximize learning. While acknowledging that this recommendation represents a daunting challenge, Schumann nonetheless sums up his neurobiological perspective on affect and ELT by claiming that language teaching must "resonate with the learner's neural system that subserve appraisal and learning," otherwise it will "frustrate achievement and ... demotivate" (p. 40).

The role of language teachers in creating a conducive affective climate is also taken up in by Dornyei and Malderez (1999) in the same collection. Like Arnold and Brown (1999), these authors are concerned not only with "what goes on 'inside'" individual learners, but also "what goes on 'between people'" in classrooms (p. 156). They posit a relationship between affect and group dynamics, claiming that "group-related issues" are central to the affective dimension of the L2 learning process (p. 156).

Teachers' responsibility in this approach is "establishing a solid 'affective group ground'" (p. 157) by applying their knowledge of group dynamics, including group formation, intermember relations, group norms, group goals, and group cohesiveness. According to Dornyei and Malderez, for optimal group development and functioning to occur in classrooms, teachers should adopt a democratic leadership style, including sharing leadership with students, making way for them to make decisions about matters affecting them (p. 165). From an affective point of view, the authors claim that teachers' democratic leadership yields "... friendlier communication" (p. 166) as well as more group-orientedness, and better member–leader relationships. Along these lines, the authors conclude that a focus on group dynamics makes "classroom events less threatening and more predictable" and "puts the excitement back into teaching" (p. 169).

As this overview of cognitive approaches to emotions in ELT texts shows, the overarching concern is maximizing learning by taking affect into account. The authors' shared assumption is that teachers who help reduce students' negative emotions and augment positive ones will increase both the amount and quality of learning, though Schumann's work departs from this binary. In addition, the authors claim that teachers who commit themselves to their own and their students' "emotional competence" (Arnold and Brown 1999, p. 24) will not only increase language learning, but also facilitate "more holistic development of our students as individuals and as responsible participants in a healthy society" (p. 24)

Sociocultural Approaches to Emotions in English Language Teacher Education

Emotions have also been addressed by Paula Golombek, Karen Johnson, Donald Freeman, and other teacher educators in ELT. These authors aim to reconceptualize the knowledge base of language teacher education by questioning the field's exclusive attention to language and language acquisition. Their reforms shift the focus away from "students as learners of language" toward "teachers as learners of language teaching" (Freeman and Johnson 1998, p. 407). They reject the conventional view of English language teachers as novices who absorb the latest methods and research findings and then, acting as conduits, pass this knowledge along to their students. Instead they propose a model of teachers as intellectuals, thinkers, and learners who study teaching and learning on the job. In this paradigm, teachers create knowledge as they teach, making sense of what they learned in their teacher education courses in light of classroom experiences and their personal histories, in an ongoing intellectual and affective process. This shift from teachers as novices to teachers as intellectuals influences Golombek's, Johnson's, and Freeman's proposals for teacher education programs in ways discussed next.

Freeman and Johnson (1998) theorize teachers as "teacher-learners" or "learners of language teaching" (p. 407). This is a way to legitimize "teachers' ways of knowing" (p. 312), also described as "insider knowledge" (Johnson 2006, p. 241) teachers acquire in their classrooms and schools. This insider knowledge includes multiple levels and layers of understanding "of learners, culture, class, gender, literacy, social issues, institutions, communities, and curricula" (Johnson and Golombek 2002, p. 3). In these authors' research, insider knowledge also involves the emotional content of teachers' learning and knowledge, revealed through teachers' stories.

The sociocultural approach taken by these teacher educators is grounded in Vygotsky's developmental theories. Accordingly, they posit learning as a "dynamic social activity," rather than an internal mental process, and knowledge as "lived practices" rather than stored information (Johnson 2006, p. 237). Narrative is the primary means they use to study L2 teachers' dynamic learning processes and knowledge because teachers' stories reveal how they "participate in and constitute their social reality" (Golombek and Johnson 2004, p. 309). Teachers' narratives offer "situated accounts of local responses to particularly sited sociocultural issues in teacher learning" (Freeman and Johnson 1998, p. 404).

Based on Vygotsky's notion that internal control is achieved when external social activity is internalized, narrative is seen as a "culturally developed tool" (Golombek and Johnson 2004, p. 310) mediating the teacher development process. Using narrative inquiry, teachers engage in a dialogic process through which they may transform both their teaching activities and their understanding of themselves as teachers.

Reviewing research on teacher narratives, Johnson and Golombek (2003) claim that writing their stories allowed teachers to "create a temporary *other*," enabling them to move from "externalized social activity to internal control over their cognitive and emotional states" (p. 734). An example of a teacher gaining internal control over her cognition and emotions can be found in Verity's (2000) discussion of her experience as an American teaching in Japan.

A confident and seasoned teacher of English in the US, Verity had been accustomed to "teaching off" (p. 182) her students; that is, relying on verbal and non-verbal student feedback to guide her in how to proceed during lessons. However, her well-honed skill of "teaching as responsive assistance in practice" (p. 183) was not relevant in the Japanese context, causing Verity to become disoriented and distressed. Analyzing her experience from a Vygotskian developmental perspective, Verity states that she found herself reverting to a "novice-like search for external mediation to regain control" (p. 183) of her teaching activity.

However, by keeping a journal while teaching in Japan, Verity was able to create a voice for herself, a temporary other, through which she could reconcile the dissonance between her "emotions as a novice" with the "cognition of an expert" (p. 183). Daily journal writing and reviewing her writing were means of reintegrating her cognitive and "affective proficiency" (p. 183), leading to a more appropriate teaching style in the new context.

Verity's research, and that of teacher educators taking a sociocultural approach, assumes that emotions should be attended to in ELT because they are central to teachers' ways of knowing. However, despite this assumption, neither emotions nor affect are explicitly theorized in this literature. They are, instead, simply mentioned as either triggers or partners of thought. The lack of attention given to theorizing emotions is surprising given the careful theorizing of learning and knowledge in this literature. Though the goals of reconceptualizing teacher education are made clear and the sociocultural assumptions about teaching and learning are made explicit, the complexity of emotions is not taken up. Instead, they are referred to monolithically, such as Golombek and Johnson's (2004) claim that an important contribution of narrative-based teacher research "has been the recognition of emotional, moral, and relational dimensions" (p. 308). Verity's statement that "affect is, by being enmeshed with cognition, inextricably linked to context as well" (p. 181) is another example of glossing over the complexity of affect.

A less totalizing use of affect and emotion and a more careful explanation of how they figure into sociocultural theory would be helpful in understanding how they relate to teacher learning and knowledge: Are they internal states? Are they an aspect of external social activity? Are they bodily sensations? Are they static? Do they change? Answers to these questions are not provided. Instead, a shared understanding of emotions is assumed.

Despite a lack of theorizing however, there is a sense in this literature that emotions are considered "outside-in" (Ahmed 2004a, p. 8), a contrast to the cognitive approach of inside-out. For example, in discussing several narratives, Golombek and Johnson (2004) describe teachers' growing awareness of contradictions between their current teaching practice and what they wanted to achieve as teachers, in some cases influenced by what they had been taught in their teacher education courses.

Awareness of conflicts between the aspirations they had cultivated through their coursework and their actual classroom practice is reported by the teachers to have triggered an emotional response, such as anxiety, fear, or dissatisfaction. Experiencing the intensity of these emotions led the teachers to resolve the contradictions by talking to a trusted colleague or writing narratives. By talking and/or writing (described as creating a temporary other), the teachers reflected on, and in some cases changed, their teaching to reconcile the perceived contradictions.

For example, one teacher, Michael, became aware of contradictions between his belief in the importance of classroom interaction, a central assumption of his education courses, and his actual domineering style with the fifth graders he was teaching. Discussing this contradiction with a colleague, or temporary other, Michael alleviated "the affective distress he was feeling," allowing him to "regain self-regulation" (Golombek and Johnson 2004, p. 319). In other words, he resolved the "emotional dissonance that drove his inquiry" (p. 319) by articulating the contradictions and experimenting with instructional strategies that were congruent with his previously-acquired beliefs about good teaching. This is a clear illustration of an outside-in approach to emotions.

According to Golombek and Johnson (2004), then, a sociocultural approach to language teacher education serves to "bring emotions to the surface as teachers recognize contradictions in their teaching" (p. 325). By telling and/or writing their stories, teachers work through the contradictions and "move from external social activity to internal control over their cognitive and emotional states" (p. 324). Despite the clarity of this formulation, however, the authors acknowledge that questions remain about how to conceptualize emotions in this important but under-theorized area of research in the sociocultural literature. To address this concern, Golombek and Johnson (2004) call for exploration of "the social origins of affect and its relationship to cognition" (p. 311). This is an area I address in Chapter 3 in my discussion of various theories of emotion and affect in critical theory, in fields other than ELT.

Multidiscplinary Approach to Emotions and Multilingualism

Aneta Pavlenko's research on emotions and multilingualism is not part of the ELT literature, being focused neither on English nor on language teaching. Nonetheless, I summarize it briefly in this chapter because Pavlenko is a prominent applied linguist and excluding her research on language and emotions, an important contribution to the applied linguistics literature, would be an obvious omission. It is interesting to note that though Pavlenko's work is often associated with sociocultural theory, she took a different direction in her research on bilinguals' use of emotion words, preferring a multidisciplinary approach. Therefore examining this research offers yet another perspective on how emotions might be theorized in their relationship to language use.

Pavlenko's (2005) overarching goal in carrying out this research was to challenge the "pervasive monolingual bias" (p. 5) of language research by replacing it with "messy, heteroglossic, and multilingual" (p. xii) linguistics. According to Pavlenko, one way to counter "militant monolingualism" (p. xiii) is by using a multilingual lens to explore language use and emotions. Training this lens on the use of emotion words and expressions informed her inquiry into whether multilinguals have "a single set of unitary emotions" or multiple "affective repertoires" (p. xiii), each mapped onto one of the user's languages.

Though Pavlenko sought to transform the language research agenda by using a multilingual lens and exploring the relationship between multiple language use and emotions, these were not her sole objectives. She also aimed to bring introspective data to bear in answering a series of interrelated questions about emotions and multilingualism, the principle ones being:

> 1) do some bi- and multilinguals feel that they become different people when they change languages? 2) how do they make sense of these perceptions? 3) what prompts some bi- and multilinguals to see their language selves as different, while others claim to have a single self?
>
> (Pavlenko, 2006, p. 6)

To explore these questions, Pavlenko and co-researcher Jean-Marc Dewaele developed a web-based questionnaire eliciting multilinguals' perceptions of the ways in which their language use intersected with emotions. Their sample included 1,039 respondents, mostly "well-educated 'elite bilinguals'" (Pavlenko 2005, p. 40). In addition to the questionnaire data, Pavlenko examined published texts of multilingual writers who had described their composing processes in more than one language. She also considered a variety of psychological, linguistic, and anthropological studies focused on language use and emotions.

In terms of theorizing emotions, Pavlenko (2005) avoided committing to any particular stance, due to her concerns about the "limitations of any single conceptual lens" (p. 43). Given her preference for a kaleidoscopic view of the relationship between emotions and multilingualism and her belief that "there is no coherent story to be told" (p.42), Pavlenko kept her theoretical options open, allowing her to consider a variety of linguistic data from different perspectives. She nonetheless acknowledges that there are separate theoretical camps in emotions research, including the universalist and the relativist. Yet, rather than subscribing to any one, Pavlenko takes a "componential or process view of emotions" (p. 80), accepting emotions "both as inner states and as relational phenomena" (p. 82), embracing what seem to be opposing positions: the universalist view of emotions as innate and biological and therefore shared by all humans; and the relativist view of emotions as socially constructed.

To reconcile the universalist and relativist perspectives, Pavlenko focused not on emotions per se, but rather on emotion concepts. These are defined as "prototypical scripts" formed as a result of "repeated experiences and that involve causal antecedents, appraisals, physiological reactions, consequences, and means of regulation and display" (p. 81). In this definition, emotion concepts are not only linguistically- and culturally-constructed phenomena learned in particular social contexts, but also physiological states that are "encoded in the limbic system" (p. 81).

In Ahmed's (2004a) terms, Pavlenko has taken both outside-in and inside-out stances in her discussion of emotion concepts. Her rationale for this dual stance is that, though she wanted to take bodies into account by acknowledging that emotions are experienced physiologically, she also wanted to avoid positing one-to-one correspondences between physical states and emotion concepts. Therefore, social explanations were required to account for how speakers learn to choose from the available linguistic and conceptual options in naming, expressing, and interpreting inner states.

It is interesting to note, however, that despite Pavlenko's claim to have adopted both universalist and relativist perspectives, her approach is actually discourse-based when she discusses findings from the web-based question, "Do you feel like a different person sometimes when you use your different languages?" (Pavlenko 2006, p. 6). To analyze the respondents' descriptions of their feelings, Pavlenko uses a Bakhtinian framework, aiming to identify multiple discourses represented in respondents' answers to the question about the relationship between language use and selves.

Pavlenko's main interest, in analyzing respondents' claim that they felt like a different person when using different languages, was to determine the sources to which they attributed those feelings of difference. Her thematic analysis of the sources revealed the following four: linguistic and cultural differences; distinct learning contexts; different levels of language and emotionality; and different levels of language proficiency (p. 10).

To give an example of her analysis, when summarizing the findings of the language and emotionality theme, Pavlenko focused on respondents' reporting that their first language was "real" and "natural" while later learned ones were "fake" and "artificial" (p. 18). Extrapolating from these data that the respondents were drawing on the Jungian distinction between "private self and *persona*" (p. 18), Pavlenko hypothesizes that "speaking one's first language stems from superior mastery of the language, whereas the perception of artificiality stems from the need to manipulate less familiar repertoires of languages later in life" (p. 19). Comparing these results to the published texts of multilingual authors, Pavlenko concludes that there are differences in users' emotional engagement with languages learned earlier and later in life. Yet, she concedes that those learned earlier are not necessarily those "favored for emotional expression"(p. 23) nor are second languages always ones of detachment.

Reviewing Pavlenko's research on emotions and multilingualism, Kramsch (2008) raises an important theoretical issue that is pertinent to the discussion of emotions and ELT in the present book. Kramsch acknowledges Pavlenko's stated desire to sidestep the universalist/relativist debate and avoid a consistent theoretical stance regarding emotions. Yet, she claims that Pavlenko nonetheless adopted an implicit poststructuralist stance, offering as evidence that Pavlenko's data analysis focused on how emotions are conceptualized through language. In fact, Kramsch applauds this position and urges greater attention to other symbolic systems, such as electronic and cinematic ones, to discover their impact on multilinguals' emotional lives. Her recommendation for future research is to study speakers' "invisible, unspeakable and untranslatable memories or prior lives lived in different languages" (p. 178), including emotions evoked through contact with various symbolic systems, and how those emotions are verbalized in their multiple languages. Yet, while urging this type of future research, Kramsch cautions against "one-to-one mapping of language X onto culture Y" (p. 177), given the postmodern diasporic world of global flows and deterritorialization.

Embodied Self in Foreign Language Learning

Kramsch's (2009) own work on the multilingual subject aims to correct what she sees as a serious gap in the foreign language teaching literature: the neglect of "affective resonances in the bodies of speakers and hearers" (p. 2). Questioning the traditional goal of getting students to speak and write like a native speaker, however that is defined, she instead proposes encouraging and valuing students' unpredictable subjectivities that may form as they engage with additional languages. Kramsch claims that an exclusive focus on native-like proficiency obscures other benefits, such as identities students may construct for themselves by adopting another language, regardless of their level of proficiency.

Kramsch explores the neglected aspects of foreign language learning, the "embodied perceptions, memories, and emotions of speakers" (p. 5), through three different data sources: language memoirs of writers, such as Jean-Paul Sartre, and Richard Rodriguez; linguistic autobiographies of foreign language learners; and metaphors used by foreign language undergraduate students to describe their language acquisition process. These different data sets were means of discovering ways in which minds and bodies connected for these learners. She explored evidence that learners became more attuned to their bodies when making unfamiliar sounds and utterances. In addition she looked at the feelings they expressed about these mind/body connections and their notions about new identities as speakers of additional languages. In other words, Kramsch is interested in both the embodied self and languages as symbolic systems to which preconceptions and stereotypes attach and how these ideas intersect with bodies.

For example, in analyzing Richard A. Watson's memoir of learning French, she points to his description of strong emotions, such as fear and disappointment, as well as his metaphors of physical pain, as in likening his attempts to speak the target language to plunging naked into cold water. As to his identity, Watson faced his own resistance to uttering certain French sounds as threatening to his preconceived notions of masculinity. These sounds required pursing the lips, a move he found constricting and diminishing and, therefore, feminine. His resistance to making these sounds, however, was not just physical and emotional but also social and historical, due to associations he made between tightening and pursing the lips and what he saw as feminized portrayals of males in French movies he disdained.

To further explore the "embodied dimension of the language learning experience" (p. 57), Kramsch surveyed 953 learners of 14 different foreign languages at the University of California, Berkeley. The survey included the following prompt, meant to get at their metaphors for language learning, thereby revealing how language might be embodied for the respondents:

> How would you describe your experience learning a foreign language? Choose a phrase, an expression, or a metaphor that best captures your experience learning to speak and write in this language.
>
> 1. Learning a language is like …
> 2. Speaking this language is like …
> 3. Writing in this language is like …
>
> (Kramsch, 2009, p. 58)

She organized the responses, characterized overall as displaying "an inordinately diverse range of embodiments of the self" (p. 60), into the following categories: challenging the body's physical limitations; escaping the limits of one's skin; the experience of biological time; pain at not being able to anticipate the future; physical experience of embodied change; enhancing the self; becoming a trickster of language; breaking spatial boundaries; and the reflexive self. Summarizing the results of the survey, Kramsch claims that foreign language learning "makes these students more conscious of their bodies (emotions, feelings, appearance, memories, fantasies)" (p. 66).

Two things are particularly notable about this statement. One is that Kramsch describes bodies as comprised of, or defined by, an interplay of physical, emotional, and mental events. The other is that she theorizes emotions and feelings as distinct, unlike other theorists I've discussed in this chapter, who don't take up feelings at all. Kramch attributes the distinction she draws between emotions and feelings to Antonio Damasio, a neuroscientist who has argued, following Spinoza, that the mind and body are inseparable. According to Kramsch's reading of Damasio's theory, emotions precede feelings. Emotions are "unconscious neural patterns that come before (and sometimes independently of) any feeling." Feelings, on the other hand, "emerge from these neural patterns or bodymaps generated by the brain" (p. 68).

The significance of this conceptualization of the relationship between emotions and feelings for Kramsch is that it helps theorize the symbolic complexity of embodied meaning-making. Meaning, according to this somatic theory, is grounded in neural patterns rather than experiences themselves. Bodies don't remember experiences, but rather neural patterns associated with them. According to Kramsch these neural patterns are the basis of symbolic meaning-making practices both objectively and subjectively: " they respond both to the fragmented time of objective reference and to the holistic time of subjective memory and imagination" (p. 70).

As I'll show in the next chapter, Kramsch's interest in the relationship between bodymaps and symbolic meaning-making differs from that of critical affective theorists who explore the relationship between affect and social change. However, for Kramsch's purposes somatic theory serves to bring together emotions, bodies, and memories in a robust way. In fact, I find her research on language learning metaphors as indicators of embodiment so compelling that I replicated it with language acquisition students and English language learners, described in Chapter 6.

Under-Theorized Emotions in Critical Applied Linguistics Research

Given that critical applied linguistics (CAL) is known for its attention to theory, it is somewhat surprising that emotions remain under-theorized in its literature. This is not to say that emotions are entirely absent; rather they sometimes appear statically, as part of the description of data, but in a parallel relationship to theory rather than fully interwoven. Before discussing this situation more completely, I'll give some background on CAL, the area in which I work.

CAL began to emerge in the 1990s as a response to the complexities of language use, learning, and teaching in a globalizing world. Dissatisfied with AL's often generic descriptions of learners and structuralist notions of language, critical applied linguists have been influenced by poststructural and critical theories (Pennycook 2001). They seek to address relationships between language and power, broadening the teaching/learning context to include sociopolitical dimensions. CAL also aims to make language learning and teaching more responsive to changes in the globalizing world, including deterritorialization, by addressing social inequality and injustice. Therefore one rich area of exploration in CAL is identity; that is, students' and teachers' complex and overlapping identities, including how race, gender, ethnicity, age, and so on, intersect with each other and with teaching and learning.

As I discussed in Chapter 1, critical applied linguistics has not completely overlooked emotions, but rather referred to them in passing, in the context of criticality and identity. A missing element has been more explicit theorizing of how emotions are linked to power and how they are embodied. To get at ways that CAL might deepen its discussion of emotions, I offer an example, Goldstein (2008), of research in which power and affect were linked, albeit loosely. This somewhat tentative link may signal the beginning of a correction to CAL's under-theorizing of emotions.

Goldstein sought to discover how students from Hong Kong used both English and Cantonese to achieve academic success. The research setting was a highly regarded Toronto high school enrolling mainly middle and upper-middle-class students, 86 percent of whom were immigrants to Canada. Goldstein's four-year ethnographic study included interviews with teachers, students, and parents as well as classroom observations and examination of school policy documents. One finding was that there was widespread objection on the part of teachers and administrators to the use of languages other than English in classrooms, hallways, and the cafeteria. In fact, a school policy report declared that, "English should not only be the language of instruction, but also the language spoken at school" (p. 212).

To make matters even more complicated, the school board which oversaw the high school published a language policy in direct contradiction to the school's language policy. Both appeared at about the same time. The school board policy called for a balanced approach to language use, one that explicitly "legitimized student multilingualism" (p. 214). According to Goldstein, the two policies revealed contradictory desires: "a local desire for institutional English monolingualism and a school board desire for student multilingualism that acknowledges English as the legitimate language of school instruction" (p. 214). These contradictions were the backdrop for students to develop their own strategies regarding which language to use and when, to further their aims of academic and social success.

Goldstein discovered that students' linguistic strategies consisted of using both Cantonese and "attentive silence" (p. 224). The interplay of these two are what she regards as cultivating "peer social capital" (p. 219), her addition to Bourdieu's notion of social capital. The use of Cantonese created solidarity with peers, cementing relationships that were essential to academic success. Cantonese-speaking students who used English with other Hong Kong students might have been considered elitist and therefore shunned, thereby losing the peer assistance they required to perform well in their studies.

These students' language use choices, according to Goldstein, were grounded in political realities in Hong Kong where only the very wealthy (or those achieving high scores on public examinations) could afford private secondary and postsecondary schooling in English. Goldstein's interviewees considered speaking English to be a form of "showing off" (p. 220) because they associated it with an elite social class of bilinguals in Hong Kong. Not only would using English signal membership in this elite class, but also create distance between the speaker and students of varying levels of English proficiency: that is, varying amounts of linguistic capital. Due to the interdependence of the students, who relied on each other for social and academic support, the wisest choice was to speak Cantonese with peers and remain attentively quiet in class. They avoided answering their teachers' questions for fear of being viewed as showing off.

However, the choice to use Cantonese and silence was not problem-free. Several dilemmas arose: insufficient opportunities to practice speaking English, itself associated with greater political and economic capital; and alienating teachers and students who preferred not hearing languages other than English spoken in the school. This meant that students were faced with tough, if not impossible, linguistic choices. If they spoke Cantonese in classes where teachers preferred English, they "risked their teachers' displeasure and disapproval" (p. 223). If they spoke Cantonese in English-only classrooms they risked punishment. In fact if they spoke Cantonese at all, in any classroom, they "risked the anger and resentment of classmates who felt excluded from their conversation" (ibid). On the other hand, "using English with Cantonese speakers was also costly" (ibid).

The struggle around these dilemmas is a highlight of Goldstein's analysis because it demonstrates the interplay of power and emotions in a rich context of the global flow of immigrant students from Hong Kong to Canada. However, though Goldstein connects power and emotions, more could be done to theorize the contradictory desires and emotional risks she uncovered by following Ahmed's (2004a) proposal to explore "how emotions circulate between bodies, examining how they 'stick' as well as move" (p. 4). This formulation offers two theoretical constructs that might benefit CAL: emotions are embodied and emotions are not static, but move and stick.

Lo (2009) shows how these constructs might inform CAL research in her analysis of constructions of disrespectful student behavior in a Korean heritage language school in the US. Pertinent to the current discussion, Lo found that teachers distinguished respectful and disrespectful classroom behavior through their reading of "students' bodily demeanor" (p. 118). By observing classroom interactions and examining teacher narratives, Lo discovered that bodily comportment, such as eye gaze, rate of breath, crying, silence, posture, gait, and so on, were considered by teachers to be indexical of either respect or disrespect. Not only were teachers attentive to these features of student bodily comportment, but they also reacted affectively to them, and often in an overt manner. When the features were read as disrespectful, teachers made their unhappiness clear to students, upbraiding them and holding them responsible for the unhappiness.

Lo offers several compelling examples of teacher/student interactions in which a teacher denounced what she viewed as inappropriate demeanor, read as disrespect, leading to "a spiraling sequence of negative emotions" in the teacher (p. 223) or a "recursive cycle of bad feelings" (p. 229). In Lo's analysis, emotions are not static, but move and stick and they are embodied, offering an important model for future studies in various contexts.

Conclusion: Departing from the Approaches Described in this Chapter

To distinguish the approach I take toward emotions in this book from those discussed in this chapter, I offer a short explanation of how each differs from mine.

Cognitive Approaches

There are two major concerns about cognitive approaches. One is that the utilitarian notion of emotions as being either beneficial or detrimental to language learning belies the complexity of emotions and learning. Sorting emotions into negative and positive categories leads to a priori judgments, e.g., anxiety is bad; enthusiasm is good; about what is required for language learning, overlooking contextual differences, and shifting emotions.

The second concern is that, due to their inattention to social contexts, cognitive approaches fail to consider that unhappiness, fear, anger, and other so-called negative emotions may be legitimate expressions of learners' difficult life situations, particularly given the challenging conditions of globalization affecting diasporic students.

By aiming to reduce what are viewed as negative emotions, so as to get on with the business of language teaching, cognitive approaches have the potential to trivialize or dismiss students' appropriate reactions to unfavorable situations and conditions, in the name of emotional intelligence. This tendency to legislate correct emotions or urge students to abandon what are perceived to be negative feelings also sabotages a possibly dynamic source of learning.

For example, if I were to try to persuade my students to develop an exclusively positive attitude toward literacy testing I would not only distance myself from their pain, but also lose the opportunity to engage them in exploring the politics of testing and its relationship to public funding for education. They might therefore be unable to see the relationship between their justifiably strong emotional reactions to exclusion and the larger social context. They might be left with the impression that their unhappiness about the tests and their failing marks were due to their emotional and linguistic failings.

These two interacting concerns point to an overarching problem: teaching and learning in the cognitive paradigm are seen as taking place in self-contained students sitting in self-contained classrooms. This framework ignores the regulation and monitoring of students and teachers in the institutions where they meet and the complex globalizing world they inhabit. A theory of power might explain the impact of regulations, such as tests, credits, pre-requisites, and grades, on students' and teachers' emotional lives, as well as ways they are resisted. Instead, in the cognitive paradigm, individual teachers are charged with inculcating emotional literacy and dispelling negative emotions, a reductive proposal given the emotional complexities of language acquisition in the neoliberal age of public sector defunding and the globalized world of diasporic flows and deterritorialization.

Sociocultural Approaches

The main concern about those who have adopted sociocultural approaches to teacher education is that they have not yet gone far enough in theorizing emotions; an omission they have conceded. Instead, they present emotions statically, as effects of dissonance between what students learned in education courses and their experience as teachers. Though this literature offers robust accounts of teachers' Vygotskian explorations, including how they acted on emotional dissonance, a more embodied and dynamic approach to emotions would give these narratives even greater resonance.

Pavlenko's Multidisciplinary Approach

Pavlenko sought to add complexity to discussions of multilingualism by eliciting emotion words connected to the different languages used by her research subjects. In addition, her Bakhtinian analyses of responses to questions about multiple languages use are speculative, leaving room for a nuanced discussion of emotions, as shifting, different from the more static conceptualizations found in cognitive analyses. Also, Pavlenko's acknowledgment of emotions as embodied, though not always clearly demonstrated in her discussion of data, is a welcome departure from those who leave out the body altogether. Though she is not concerned with English language teaching, her research is an important contribution to the study of the relationship between language and emotions.

Like Pavlenko, I have chosen to sacrifice theoretical consistency to be able to take up multiple lenses with which to examine my data. Thus, I call upon both feminist conceptualizations of emotions as political and embodied and Deleuzian notions of affect as embodied and unencumbered, a source of possibility.

Kramsch's Embodied Self

Kramsch's research comes closest to my own in terms of bringing the body to second language acquisition. However, unlike Kramsch I'm more interested in pedagogy itself than in the possible benefits of multilingualism to those studying additional languages. Also Kramsch does not bring critical theory to bear in her analysis, but instead relies on Damasio's neurobiological theory to explain mind/body connections. In the next chapter I explore theories that conceptualize emotions not as neural patterns, but, rather, as socially constructed dimensions of human experience.

Critical Applied Linguistics

"Struggle" is a word that often appears in the CAL literature. Identities, classrooms, languages, and learning are described as sites of struggle, a way to acknowledge unequal power and resistance to power in social contexts. However, though struggle suggests pain, the embodied nature of struggle is rarely taken up; one exception being the work of Lo (2009), discussed in this chapter. Given the importance attached to theory in CAL, I foresee greater interest in theorizing emotions in the future, both the fluid and dynamic aspects of shifting emotions and their embodiment. This will necessitate an "affective turn" in CAL, to which this book aims to contribute. The next chapter looks at how the affective turn has influenced other fields with an eye toward how it might be adopted in CAL.

3
CRITICAL THEORIES OF AFFECT AND EMOTIONS

> A model of emotions that takes their complexity as everyday concepts seriously would see them as experiences that we recognize as involving both cultural meaning and bodily feeling. While they are subjectively felt and interpreted, it is socialized human beings – that is, thinking human bodies – who are feeling them in specific social contexts.
>
> (Leavitt, 1996, p. 531)

> The challenge of the perspective of the affects resides primarily in the syntheses it requires. This is, in the first place, because affects refer equally to the body and the mind; and, in the second, because they involve both reason and passion. Affects require us, as the term suggests, to enter the realm of causality, but they offer a complex view of causality because the affects belong simultaneously to both sides of the causal relationship. They illuminate, in other words, both our power to affect the world around us and our power to be affected by it, along with the relationship between these two powers.
>
> (Hardt, 2007, p. ix)

One way to begin theorizing emotions or affect in critical English language teaching is to ask what they offer, including what areas of investigation are opened up.[1] However, before getting to these issues, it is important to establish how emotions are being theorized in this book, given the various lenses that can be used to examine them critically. To that end, I begin the chapter with a review of literatures on the "affective turn" in critical theory across such fields as anthropology, education, gender studies, geography, media studies, philosophy, and sociology. This review includes a discussion of how affect, emotion, and the relationship between them are theorized by affective-turn writers, including Patricia T. Clough and Brian Massumi. The discussion of terminology is followed by an examination of the treatment of emotions in current feminist scholarship, including the work of Sara Ahmed, Lauren Berlant, and Sianne Ngai.

In the final sections of the chapter I turn to examples of how emotions have been treated in various critical teaching contexts, including the work of Christa Albrecht-Crane and Michalanos Zemblyas. The concluding section examines how I plan to apply emotions to critical English language teaching in subsequent chapters.

Theorizing Affect/Emotions Critically: The Affective Turn in Critical Theory

Influence of Spinoza and Deleuze

Though the authors whose work I review in this chapter are from different fields and therefore have varying concerns, all have been influenced by the seventeenth-century philosopher Baruch Spinoza and the twentieth-century philosopher Gilles Deleuze. Spinoza and Deleuze are often evoked, though interpretations and applications of their work vary.

Despite a lack of uniformity in applying Spinoza and Deleuze, one feature connecting the work cited in this chapter is a grounding in Spinoza's critique of Rene Descartes' dualism: his separation of mind and body. The authors all incorporate affect and/or emotions as a challenge to the tradition in scholarly research of positing a division between a rational mind and a feeling body, one that has sequestered or avoided affect so as not to contaminate what are claimed to be objective research findings. By focusing on Spinoza's and Deleuze's theories of affect, current affective-turn theorists aim to bridge mind and body, thinking and feeling, reason and passion. This is not to say that mind and body in this literature are merged. Rather, their connection is viewed as a way to open up new possibilities of thinking and problem solving.

Leavitt (1996), an anthropologist, for example, claims that the "bridging character" of emotions makes them both useful in daily life and "simultaneously 'hard to think' in most theoretical discourse" (p. 517). This statement acknowledges the usefulness and complexity of emotions while urging their incorporation into critical theory despite, or perhaps because of, the difficulty of pinning them down.

According to Morgan (2006), an editor of Spinoza's work, Descartes isolated the mind from the body to preserve certain theological beliefs, including "free will and the immortality of the soul" (p. ix). Spinoza, on the other hand, challenged this isolation by proposing a concept of mind/body as connected, "a whole in which physical events and mental ones are. ... related, but separate" (p. x). The relationship, as Spinoza saw it, was that mind and body are composed of the same substance. Included in his "passion for unity and totality" (p. xi) was an understanding of emotions "as psychological correlates of physical states of the human body" (p. 2).

Deleuze championed Spinoza's work, bringing mind/body connections to contemporary philosophy. Deleuze's influence on the affective turn is mainly seen in his assumptions about the role of philosophical thinking as well as three key concepts: lines of flight; becoming; and the body without organs. Reacting against the notion of philosophy as a search for underlying fundamental truths, Deleuze instead saw it as an opportunity to "giv[e] form to the chaos of life" (Colebrook 2002, p. 13). The goal was not to understand what is observable or discover what is hidden, but rather to enter the virtual world of possibility. Possibility is "an effective striving in life: to enhance its power, to maximise what it can do," a departure from life as a "progression of ordered sequences" (p. 57). Thinking is nomadic, untethered, capable of soaring into "lines of flight," allowing "time to take off on a new path" as "disruptions, breaks, new beginnings" (p. 57). Central to Deleuze's investigation of the virtual and possible is his concept of becoming, a formlessness in which binaries, such as woman/man, teacher/student, animal/human, and pre-given identities, don't apply.

Affect and becoming for Deleuze are related to his concept of the body without organs, that is, the non-organic unjudged body in which "organs are no longer anything more than intensities that are produced, flows, thresholds, and gradients" (Deleuze and Guattari 1987, p. 164). As we'll see in the discussion of the affective turn in critical theory, these theorists are drawn to the concept of the body as indeterminate because it acknowledges the potential for humans to affect and be affected in unpredictable ways, offering possibilities for political change. Conceptualizing lines of flight, becoming, and the body without organs is a reaction against predetermined structures and identities and an orientation toward indeterminacy and immanence. These concepts propose a turn away from the subject as an individual with multiple identities toward "a non-unitary or nomadic vision of selves as inter-relational forces" (Braidotti 2005). However, we'll also see that while some insist on the autonomy of affect, in a move away from poststructuralism, others blur the lines between affect and emotions and retain poststructural assumptions about identity and power.

Distinguishing Affect and Emotions: Autonomy of Affect

While affective-turn theorists share an interest in Spinoza's and Deleuze's non-dualistic philosophies, they differ in how they theorize the relationship between affect and emotions. Some, such as Sara Ahmed and Sianne Ngai, use the terms interchangeably while others distinguish them as separate entities. I'll begin with the latter group, which includes Patricia T. Clough, a sociologist, and Brian Massumi, a political theorist/philosopher. Most notable about their contribution to the affective turn is their theorizing affect as not only distinct from emotion, but also autonomous; that is, unstructured, prelinguistic, and unqualified bodily intensities. This positing of affect as autonomous, they claim, enhances critical theory by opening up possibilities for action and change not accounted for in poststructural understandings. In other words, finding poststructuralism too deterministic in how it theorizes power's positioning of people socially, they theorize affect's vital and unencumbered potential for change.

Clough (2007), for example, distances herself from both Foucault and Butler by focusing on "the dynamism of the body" rather than on the body as a "product of cultural form or the effect of the performativity of language" (p. 8). She theorizes affect, without reference to culture or language, as the intensification or diminution of "a body's capacity to act, to engage, and to connect" (p. 2). Defining affect, in a reference to Spinoza and Deleuze, as "bodily capacities to affect and be affected," Clough also distinguishes affect and emotions, explaining their relationship in the following way: "Affect constitutes a nonlinear complexity out of which the narration of conscious states such as emotion are subtracted" (p. 2). "Non-linear" in this context is a reference to Deleuze's challenge to conventional linear thinking and his proposal for "the dynamism and instability of thought" (Colebrook 2002, p. 4). Clearly in this definition, emotions are seen as conscious and linguistic, and, therefore, secondary. In fact, Clough is uninterested in emotions per se.

An important goal of the affective turn in critical theory for Clough (2007) is to account for the impact of technology on bodies. Defining affect as "potential bodily responses. ... in excess of consciousness" (p. 2), she points out that technology can capture that which is not accessed consciously. In this way, Clough brings to critical theory ways to understand the relationships among bodies, technology, and matter, allowing for attention to the biomediated body, for example, the manufacture of genetic material. For Clough, this focus on the biomediated body represents a shift in critical theory, from a poststructural focus on discipline to a "postbiological" focus on "biopolitical control" (p. 3). Affect, in this formulation, circulates freely, "autonomous from the particular thing it embodies" (p. 4), able to "self-organize," a condition of possibility in the postbiological world.

For his part, Massumi (2002), in a challenge to poststructuralism, wonders how change is accounted for in what he views as a deterministic theory. He objects to the notion of identity constructions that "prescript every possible signifying and countersignifying move as a selection from a repertoire of possible permutations on a limited set of predetermined terms" (p. 3). As with Clough, the claim here is that poststrucutural/postmodern theories of power, positionality, and hegemony leave out the potential for transformation, or, in Massumi's terms, movement. He reacts against the theoretical construct of subject positions, characterizing them as static sites plotted out on a grid and therefore predetermined, even if multiple. In place of subject positions, Massumi proposes the moving body, "never present in position, only ever in passing" (p. 5). The body, in this conceptualization, as in Deleuze's, is indeterminate and open "to an elsewhere and otherwise than it is, in any here and now" (p. 5).

Calling upon Spinoza's theory of bodies and minds as composed of a single substance or matter, Massumi proposes "put[ting] matter unmediatedly back" into critical theory (p. 4). This engagement with unmediated bodily matter acknowledges indeterminacy and, therefore, the potential for change. The moving body is "an immediate, unfolding relation to its own nonpresent potential to vary" (p. 4). Change is thus conceptualized not as grand ruptures between past and future, but, instead, as subtle, continuous, qualitative, "felt and unforeseen" (p. 1).

Massumi connects ongoing, indeterminate bodily change or movement to affect, by bringing in Spinoza's connection between movement and sensation. According to Massumi, Spinoza described this link as "a body's *capacity* to enter into relations of movement and rest," once again the potential "to affect or be affected" (p. 15). So, for Massumi, while affect is the potential for moving bodies to act, unencumbered by power, positionality, and hegemony, emotions are the conscious naming of experiences, "the sociolinguistic fixing of the quality of an experience which is from that point onward defined as personal" (p. 28). Whereas affect is "unqualified" and therefore "not ownable or recognizable and is thus resistant to critique" (p. 28), emotions are qualifications because they register what bodies feel or "re-register an already felt state, for the skin is faster than the word" (p. 25). However, as I discuss next, not all theorists engaged with affect subscribe to this clear distinction between affect as felt and emotions as sociolinguistic fixing of feelings.

Affect and Emotions as Interchangeable

> While you can separate an affective response from an emotion that is attributed as such (the bodily sensations from the feeling of being afraid), this does not mean that in practice, or in everyday life, they are separate. In fact, they are contiguous; they slide into each other; they stick, and cohere, even when they are separated.
>
> (Ahmed, 2010, n.1)

Massumi's and Clough's insistence on the autonomy of affect has been challenged by a number of feminist scholars, including Sara Ahmed, Claire Hemmings, and Sianne Ngai. Their critique is taken up in this section to demonstrate how affect and emotion can be theorized as interchangeable, the position I take in this book. Generally speaking, critics of the autonomy of affect reject claims of affect as presocial, believing instead that it is, at least in part, socially constructed.

Ahmed (2010) challenges the view of affect as autonomous and unqualified, theorizing it, quite differently, as "what sticks, or what sustains or preserves the connection between ideas, values, and objects" (p. 230, n. 1). Affect, then, is not indeterminate and free floating, but "already in place" (ibid), already social, not presocial, even before we are affected, before "something happens that creates an impression on the skin" (ibid).

It is this already-in-place feature of affect, allowing us to be affected "in some way more than others" (ibid) that interests Ahmed because it points to links between psychic and social dimensions, offering possible explanations of "how things cohere *in a certain way*" (p. 231, n.1). A deeper appreciation of what is already in place and therefore coheres in a certain way is an entrée to political understanding and change.

In addition, Ahmed (2010) raises concerns about distinguishing affect and emotion. This split, she claims, dismisses " the work of emotions" (p. 230, n. 1), by excluding the *socialized* body with its directions and orientations. Emotions are not simply sociolinguistically fixed judgments that follow from affect, as Massumi theorizes them, but rather they "shape how bodies are moved in the worlds they inhabit" (p. 230, n.1). Given the greater importance Ahmed attaches to emotions than either Clough or Massumi, for whom affect is the theoretical focus, it stands to reason that Ahmed does not insist on their clear distinction from affect. In addition, and in contrast to Clough and Massumi, she attends more to emotions than to affect.

However, Ahmed is not interested in what emotions *are*, but rather what they *do*. She explores "how emotions circulate between bodies, examining how they 'stick' as well as move" (Ahmed, 2004a, p. 4). More particularly, she is concerned with how emotions are sorted in social contexts into good and bad, strong and weak, along gender and racial lines. To put it another way, she does not move away from poststructuralism, but instead incorporates emotions into it.

Hemmings (2005), too, challenges the claim that affect is autonomous and therefore unique in its ability to bring about change. While sympathetic to a search for the "non-socially-determined" as a source of social transformation, she questions Massumi's "theoretical celebration of affect as uniquely situated" (p. 550) in this regard. As counter-evidence she offers examples of how affect can be a "mechanism of social reproduction" (p. 551) rather than unencumbered by social structures. Her examples of "affective responses that strengthen rather than challenge a dominant social order" (p. 551) include the corporeal thrill of consumerism and the warm feelings that might be generated by membership in a fascist group. In fact, Hemmings accuses Massumi of implicitly splitting affect dualistically into good and bad, by considering only good affect, so that he can overstate his case for "the optimism of affective freedom" (p. 551).

To make her own case for linking mind and body in critical theory without recourse to affect's autonomy, Hemmings gives a reading of Deleuze that opposes the one offered by Massumi. Countering Massumi's claim that affect is presocial, Hemmings points to Deleuze's positing of an affective cycle in which intensity (body) and judgment (mind) continually affect each other. In Massumi's formulation, on the other hand, the affective cycle is body–affect–emotion, "a self-contained phrase repeated in time" (p. 564). A more accurate reading of Deleuze's affective cycle is, according to Hemmings, "an ongoing, incrementally altering chain—body–affect–emotion–affect–body—doubling back upon the body and influencing the individual's capacity to act in the world" (p. 564). Underscoring Deleuze's description of this doubling back leads Hemmings to claim that affective cycles "form *patterns* that are subject to reflective or political, rather than momentary or arbitrary, judgments" (p. 564). The potential of these affective cycles, or patterns, convinces Hemmings that "affect might in fact be valuable precisely to the extent that it is *not* [emphasis added] autonomous" (p. 565).

Sianne Ngai (2005) offers another possible way to resolve the autonomous vs. mediated affect debate. Distancing herself from Massumi's strong distinction between affect as bodily intensity and emotion as sociolinguistic fixing, she argues for a middle position. Rather than splitting affect and emotion, she theorizes their relationship as a continuum, one of "intensity or degree, rather than a formal difference of quality or kind" (p. 27). Along these lines, she refers to affect not in the singular, but in the plural (affects), sometimes calling them feelings, and describing them as "less *formed* and structured than emotions, but not lacking form or structure altogether" (p. 27).

The advantage of this position is that it allows for the type of non-linear loop proposed by Hemmings. In Ngai's formulation the analysis is of "ongoing states" from affects to emotions back to affects and so on. She describes the reciprocity between affects and emotions as a process whereby affects "acquire the semantic density and narrative complexity of emotions, and emotions conversely denature into affects" (p. 27). This fluidity between less-structured affects and more-structured emotions is consistent with Ngai's methodology in which she examines "ugly feelings" in texts across various genres, historical periods, and aesthetic traditions, discussed further in the next section.

Ugly feelings is a reference to emotions that are less popular than those that are normally examined in philosophical and psychoanalytic texts, such as anger, fear, melancholia, and shame. Ngai focuses instead on "minor and generally unprestigious feelings" (p. 6), such as irritation, envy, and paranoia.

Ngai's political project in reading a variety of texts and art works through the lens of these "minor" feelings is to interrogate restricted or obstructed agency, or, what prevents people from acting with others in their best interests, including how works of art encourage or discourage action. Her book *Ugly Feelings* looks at how feelings such as envy, especially of the disempowered for the powerful can be considered as "allegories for an autonomous or bourgeois art's increasingly resigned and pessimistic understanding of its *own* relationship to political action" (p. 3). Her goal in studying ugly feelings is to discover possible areas of resistance or what she calls "critical productivity" (p. 3). She looks at "how emotions might be recuperated for critical praxis" (p. 8).

Ngai's work is in line with a trend in feminist scholarship of attending to emotions as a way to bring the body to critical praxis. Returning to Hemmings (2005), one of her concerns about the concept of autonomous affect is that it excludes the work of these feminists as well as critical race and postcolonial scholars who attend to "emotional investments, political connectivity, and the possibility of change" (p. 557). In the next section I focus on the work of feminist scholars who examine emotions, moving toward a discussion of methodology: how emotions might be considered critically in English language teaching.

Feminist Scholarship on Emotions

> Emotions are what move us, and how we are moved involves interpretations of sensations and feelings not only in the sense that we interpret what we feel, but also in that what we feel might be dependent on past interpretations that are not necessarily made by us, but that come before us.
>
> (Ahmed, 2004a, p. 171)

A group of feminist scholars has looked at the complexity of various emotions, including envy, anxiety, compassion, happiness, and shame, by analyzing an array of print and non-print texts and works. Their shared theoretical assumptions, expressed in Ahmed's quote that opens this section are: emotions are embodied (sensations and feelings); they are shifting (we are moved), not static or monolithic; and they are socially constructed (our interpretation of them might depend on others' prior interpretations), not private, internal, or cognitive. In addition, these feminist scholars include emotions in critical theory not to reject poststructuralism, but rather to incorporate this missing dimension. Power and emotion go hand in hand, from their perspective, and the study of both, in tandem, heightens the potential for critical praxis.

In addition, by focusing on emotions, feminist scholars reclaim a rich area of research that has traditionally been considered irrelevant, irrational, and exclusively female.

To illustrate these scholars' methodologies and findings, I focus on three emotions – compassion, envy, and happiness – discussed in the following texts: Lauren Berlant's (2004a) introduction to her edited collection, *Compassion: The Culture and Politics of an Emotion;* Sianne Ngai's (2005) chapter on envy from her book, *Ugly Feelings;* and Sara Ahmed's (2010) examination of happiness, *The Promise of Happiness.* Berlant and Ngai are English professors working in the US; Ahmed is a professor of race and cultural studies in a media and communications department in the UK. When analyzing a particular emotion, they rely not only on literary texts, but also news reports, court documents, films, paintings, television shows, psychoanalytic texts, literary criticism, and historical documents. Their analyses move skillfully between emotions as bodily experiences and socio-historical constructions, laying bare complexities and contradictions, and implying, or overtly suggesting, how the analysis might be a means of political action. That is, they are essays of engagement.

Compassion

Berlant (2004a) introduces her collection *Compassion: The Culture and Politics of an Emotion* with an essay, "Compassion (and withholding)", a title signaling complexity and contradiction at the outset. In this introductory essay she situates her treatment of compassion historically by contrasting features of the platforms of two US Presidents: Lyndon Johnson's Great Society in the 1960s and George W. Bush's faith-based "compassionate conservatism" in the 1990s. The aim of this contrast is not to favor one over the other, or to restate the most obvious differences between them through the conventional liberal vs. conservative reading. Rather, Berlant uses the two political platforms as examples of how compassion is connected to "ongoing debates about the ethics of privilege" (p. 1). These debates have cropped up throughout US history due to the gap between the promise of equality and actual class, racial, sexual, and ethnic inequalities that belie claims of democracy. In the case of the Great Society, the aim was to redress these inequities through the "grand gestures" (p. 2) of the welfare state. "Compassionate conservatism," on the other hand, shifted the focus away from institutions to individuals, in particular, "working citizens – that is, the person who works for a living, especially for *his* [emphasis added] family's living" (p. 2).

Though different in their aims and targets, Berlant claims that underlying both the Great Society and compassionate conservatism is the problem of compassion's unavoidable connection to withholding. Compassion entails not just feeling for or with the sufferer, but also a sadistic refusal to help. There is a relationship between "becoming capaciously compassionate and becoming distant from responsibility for what one experiences directly and indirectly" (p. 10) about under-served and ostracized populations and individuals. Given the ways humans are socialized to calculate degrees of social pain, "we are being trained in stinginess, in not caring" (p. 10). The political question for Berlant, then, is: "What if it turns out that compassion and coldness are not opposite at all but are two sides of a bargain that the subjects of modernity have struck with structural inequality?" (p. 10). She finds that compassion is equally capable of offering "an alibi for an ethical or political betrayal" and "initiat[ing] a circuit of practical relief" (p. 11).

Envy

The complexity and contradictions of an emotion are also taken up by Ngai (2005) in her discussion of envy. Like Berlant, she sets aside the most obvious associations and interpretations to make her case for envy's potential as a political tool. Ngai explores and then complicates the expected attribution of envy as a feminized emotion and the attendant psychoanalytic interpretations of envy as female longing for that which she cannot have, including penis envy. These hackneyed associations, she claims, overlook what is most interesting about envy: its relationship to inequality. That is, there is often a material basis for envy, one grounded in social class inequality; ignoring this aspect strips envy of "its potential critical agency" (p. 129).

Weaving together a wide range of authors, including Freud, Spivak, Kristeva, Fanon, Jameson, Klein, and Butler, Ngai devotes the majority of the chapter to an analysis of envy in the film *Single White Female (SWF)* (1992). In it, Allie, a young middle-class woman living in New York City advertises for a roommate. She chooses Hedy, a working-class young woman, who, once she moves in, begins to emulate Allie's wardrobe, haircut, and behavior. Eventually the relationship escalates into violence culminating in Hedy stabbing Allie's boyfriend in the eye with a stiletto and Allie's murder of Hedy in self-defense.

A feminist critique of *SWF* was that it represented a backlash against solidarity between women, offered a cautionary tale for those contemplating crossing class lines, and was homophobic, given Hedy's suggested lesbianism. However, Ngai claims that objections about the antagonism between the two main characters and the violent nature of their interaction miss an opportunity to examine how homosocial groups, such as feminists, interact, including how envy is a vital component in the development of group feelings and should therefore be attended to.

To this end, Ngai examines envy in *SWF* from a different perspective, bringing in a published debate between feminist scholars Susan Gubar and Robyn Wiegman, who disagreed about the relationship between feminism and poststructuralism. Gubar, the veteran scholar, argued that poststructuralism, by aligning with race and ethnic studies, had shut out feminism. More interesting to Ngai, however, than the parameters of the debate, which fell along generational lines, was the fact that Gubar had initially titled her essay "Who killed feminist criticism?," but later changed it to, "What ails feminist critique?," a switch Gubar herself references in her article. This substitution of the more polite and depersonalized title for the more overtly violent one is an indication to Ngai of a refusal to deal directly with the pain of exclusion and intergenerational conflict. Wiegman, on the other hand, in what Ngai sees as an ironic move, begins her essay by "invoking Amanda Cross's *Murder Without a Text*, a mystery novel featuring 'a seasoned feminist scholar bludgeoning a student to death'" (p. 133).

The envy demonstrated in the exchange between Gubar and Wiegman, where Gubar implicitly worries about being left behind by younger scholars, features the type of violence found in *SWF*, albeit symbolically. The question Ngai raises regarding the symbolically violent exchange between the veteran feminist and her younger counterpart is whether antagonistic and violent images from a film such as *SWF* "can be imaginatively and provocatively used to address such disagreements from within" (p. 135). If feminists are split along the lines outlined in the Gubar/Wiegman debate, with younger feminists more inclined toward multiple identities and subject positions and the older generation advocating an exclusive focus on women, the split might best be acknowledged as enriching rather than necessarily divisive. Going back to the connection to *SWF*, Ngai concludes that the film "could be said to allegorize the state of contemporary feminism as internally divided or split, yet *held together by this very split*" (p. 168). In this formulation, envy signals an opportunity for intensified coalition building and should therefore be neither denied nor avoided, but embraced as a useful tool.

Happiness

Ahmed (2010), too, looks to film in her chapter on "Melancholic Migrants" in *The Promise of Happiness*. Like Berlant, Ahmed examines the relationship between an emotion and its opposite, in her case happiness and melancholy. As a second-generation daughter of a Pakistani Muslim father and an English Christian mother, Ahmed is interested in media portrayals of immigrants, especially the interactions between the first and second generations. She situates her discussion of melancholic migrants in the history of the British Empire, especially writers who justified empire, such as classical Utilitarians Jeremy Bentham, James Mills, and John Stuart Mills. These Utilitarian thinkers, she claims "drew on the discourses of maximizing happiness in support of the imperial mission" (p. 123).

Centered on Bentham's often-cited maxim of "the greatest happiness of the greatest number," utilitarianism, according to Ahmed, "involves the ethical injunction to maximize happiness" (p. 123) among colonized populations across the Empire. James Mills, for example, rationalized the maximize-happiness injunction by arguing that "the benefits to the colonized must be greater than the cost to the colonizer" (p. 124). Along those lines, both James Mills and his son John Stuart Mills worked for the East India Company whose existence was justified as philanthropy which would lead both to economic enhancement of the colonized and to their greater happiness. Though a profit-making company with administrative and military power, it was nonetheless considered philanthropic, a sacrifice of the colonizers in the name of the greater prosperity and happiness for the colonized. Thus, according to Ahmed, "[t]he civilizing mission can be redescribed as a happiness mission" (p. 125). For this to happen, though, "the colonized other must first be deemed unhappy" (p. 125). In this way, "the misery of native culture" (p. 125) justifies colonial rule.

Finding that these beliefs persist to this day, Ahmed claims that there is an implicit demand that contemporary migrants in the UK consider the history of empire as a history of happiness. As to their own role in that history, migrants should "accept empire as the gift of happiness" (p. 131). The gift of colonized happiness can only be appreciated if immigrants shrug off any experiences they may have of racism. Clinging to contacts with racism leads to self-imposed melancholia, an embrace of the sad past rather than the promise of a happy future. In addition to letting go of encounters with racism and other indignities, immigrants must let go of the past. If they are melancholy, they have only themselves to blame for "failing to let go of what has been lost" (p. 141) from their culture of origin. To achieve happiness, melancholic migrants must transcend loss, "which keeps them facing the wrong way"; they must be "redirected, or turned around" (p. 141).

According to Ahmed, these are precisely the moral lessons of the 2002 film, *Bend It Like Beckham* which tells the story of Jesse, the daughter of Sikh migrants, who wants to play football against her parents' wishes. From Ahmed's perspective, the film moralizes about the thwarted promise of happiness for migrants who won't let go of their lives in the old country and of racist encounters in the adopted country. If only immigrants would shrug off their past, including racist incidents, the film implicitly preaches, they could be authors of their happiness. *Bend It Like Beckham* demonstrates that to achieve happiness, immigrants must convert bad old feelings into good new ones at the individual level.

Jesse's father is the melancholic migrant who clings to the past, particularly his experience with racism when he first migrated and was excluded from playing on a cricket team because he wore a turban. At the beginning of the film, he refuses to allow Jesse to play football, to protect her from a similar wound, demonstrating melancholia by clinging to his exclusion from a team in the past. However, by the end, admitting that holding on to that old injury has caused him to suffer, he declares that "she *should play* in order not to suffer like him" (p. 142). In other words, his attachment to the wound of racism had been the reason for his suffering, not the racism itself. Once he lets it go, he and his daughter can happily enter their bright futures.

Because Ahmed theorizes emotions as "about objects, which they hence shape, and are also shaped by contact with objects" (Ahmed, 2004a, p. 7), it is interesting to look at her reading of the father's turban in *Bend It like Beckham*. The film suggests, according to Ahmed, that the father's attachment to his turban is an unhealthy tether to his culture, his religion, and his native country. By clinging to the past, he "holds on ... to what keeps him apart" as well as to "the unhappiness of difference" (p. 143). His unhappiness, in other words, is self-produced, rather than a result of racist exclusion. Thus, from the film's perspective, he had converted an object of love "into a memory of racism" (p. 143), making himself the author of his own unhappiness. He could be happy only if he would attach himself to happier objects, such as football. In fact, this is what happens at the end of the film. With her father's blessing, Jesse goes to the US to pursue her dream of becoming a professional football player, focusing her aspirations on a worthy object, seen as neutral and happy, unencumbered by her father's past.

Ahmed's interest in the relationship between objects and emotions offers a promising avenue for research on emotions in critical English language teaching. Objects such as assessment tests, dictionaries, cellphones, textbooks, and others shape and are shaped by emotions that are worth attending to because they may affect teaching and learning. Two of these "sticky" objects (Ahmed, 2004a, p. 89) and the emotions that adhere to them are examined in Chapter 4.

In the next and final section of this chapter, I will summarize the current literature on emotions/affect in critical teaching.

Critical Literature on Teachers' and Students' Emotions

> I am suggesting here that we change the pedagogic focus from identity-based relations to localized, contextual possibilities of working with what one finds *between and through* positions of identity. A focus on the dynamics of affectivity ...
>
> (Albrecht-Crane, 2005, p. 492)

A frustration about the literature on affect and emotions in critical teaching is that it is very long on theory and very short on practice. It offers extensive rationales for treating affect and/or emotions in classrooms with little or no data or examples from actual applications. Though there is significant discussion of the importance of considering emotions, few descriptions are provided of the look, sound, or feel of classrooms in which emotions were, in fact, attended to. The exceptions, however, are illuminating and point the way to possible relationships between affect/emotions and critical praxis. I will focus on three texts grounded in classroom data and/or assignments: Christa Albrecht-Crane's (2005) "Pedagogy as friendship: Identity and affect in the conservative classroom"; Marianne Grey's (2009) "Ethnographers of difference in a critical EAP community-becoming"; and Michalinos Zembylas's (2005) *Teaching with Emotion: A Postmodern Enactment*.

Albrecht-Crane's research site is a US college in what she calls a politically conservative region where Mormon culture predominates. However, rather than positioning herself in opposition to her conservative students, Albrecht-Crane adopts a stance of friendship toward them, one grounded in "the dynamics of affectivity" (p. 492). The aim of this stance is to incorporate poststructural understandings of identity, ideology, and representation as well as "the dynamics that exceed those processes" (p. 492); that is, affect. The pedagogy, then, allows for Deleuzian lines of flights that break from conventions, making room for transformative moments. Dialogue is the centerpiece through which teachers and students learn from each other, producing "new modes of being together" (p. 492). They thus move beyond the traditional teacher/student binary, not once and for all, but on unanticipated occasions that can be captured and analyzed.

The extended example Albrecht-Crane offers of new modes of being together, that is, becoming, and lines of flight, begins with an undergraduate student's written response to the following sentence from a poststructural text, *Beginning Theory* by Peter Barry:

> … meaning is always attributed to the object or idea by the human mind, and constructed by and expressed through language: it is not already contained within the things.
>
> (as cited in Albrecht-Crane, 2005, p. 505)

The student, Casey, enrolled in Albrecht-Crane's critical theory course, responded to this sentence in light of his identity as a Mormon, and of the church's teaching that the *Bible* and *The Book of Mormon* contain the truth, not as a construction or representation, but within themselves. He explained how his faith in these truths had shaped his worldview and convinced him that "the Mormon Church is the truest church on the face of the earth" (p. 505). However, and this is where Albrecht-Crane claims that a line of flight takes off, Casey goes on in his essay to raise some doubts: "There is a strong possibility that I am looking at this backwards, and that the only reason my religion does these things for me is because I have given it life and meaning through personal faith, which in itself is a construction of reality created through the mind" (p. 506).

Even more interesting to Albrecht-Crane is the next and final sentence of Casey's response: "But for my own personal belief's sake, I sure hope it's not." She reads this sentence neither as resistance to critical theory nor as acceptance, but, rather, a "non-refusal refusal" (p. 506): "[H]e knows that he cannot come over to my side, and yet he waves at me" (p. 509). Albrecht-Crane, touchingly, describes how Casey's waving threw her off, leaving her unable to write "the usual stuff in the margins" (p. 509). Her student's simultaneous compliance and resistance stymies her because he is "within the system and he exceeds it" (p. 506). She analyzes "I hope not" as a becoming, or Casey's "becoming nomadic, within his narratives of religion and community belonging" (p. 508). It is an instance of movement, passing through a place that neither rejects his identities nor takes up new ones.

After much reflection, Albrecht-Crane wrote on Casey's paper:

> Thanks for being so honest; I appreciate your generosity in your open response. Yes, these ideas are not just words, but they ask us to engage a bit deeper and evaluate what we want and desire and feel comfortable with. I like the tone and feel of your essay a lot. You make me chuckle at the end ... Can't wait to read your next paper.
>
> (p. 509)

Albrecht-Crane characterizes the exchange between her and Casey as one of interlocuteurs who have disrupted the teacher/student binary. He has "unworked" her identity as the "teacher-authority" and his student-writer identity has been "unmoored" (p. 509). After the course ends and Casey graduates, becoming a high school English teacher, he stays in touch and gives her permission to excerpt his paper in her article, saying that reading it might allow him to "stretch" (p. 509). The reference to stretching takes Albrecht-Crane back to their exchange which she characterizes as "a becoming-teacher/student, creating an alternative space of learning, writing, and education" (p. 509).

Another example of attending to affect, becoming, and lines of flight can be found in Grey's (2009) discussion of "nomadic ethnographers" in an EAP business class for international students in an Australian university. Grey aimed to carry out critical EAP by encouraging students to disrupt conventions and to "contest their own or others' positionings" (p. 124) in the business world and in the university. To this end, she had them work in groups on a diversity research project culminating in a poster to be presented to the class. They were to examine their peers' attitudes toward diversity and stereotyping through various media, including digital cameras, and mobile phones, along with pens and paper. The presentation of the poster was intended to convince their fellow students of possibilities for action in the university.

Grey regards her students' research and completed projects through the lens of affect. Discussing how they embarked on the projects, she mentions their excitement, companionship, desire, joy, as well as their uncertainty in anticipating "encounters not yet known or made" (p. 121). Her focus in the article settles on one group's poster, consisting of black and white photos of each member of the group, placed around the edges, and a large color photo in the center, of a composite face including features from each group member, a hybrid image of varying races and genders. The classroom discussion about this poster is the center of Grey's analysis. She describes students' moment-by-moment reactions to the hybrid photo, including both glee and discomfort at its disruption of conventional portraits of members of static and identifiable genders and races.

Offering a Deleuzian analysis, Grey discusses how desire circulated in the classroom as "another way to account for leakage that occurs" when students take up "multiple discourses of difference around gender, sexuality, race, religion, and so on" (p. 124).

By "leakage" she means "this overflow of bodies interacting" or "bodily meaning-making which can be joyful, sorrowful, conflictual, or insightful" (p. 124). This attention to desire at the micro-level allows Grey to train her pedagogic eye on becoming; that is, "the way difference is continually re-shaped by and through a complex, ongoing process of desiring bodies relating to one another" (p. 124). She calls for greater integration of international and local students to engage in this type of research as a way to disrupt normative discourses and literacy practices.

Zembylas (2005) offers examples not from his own teaching, but from a three-year ethnographic study of science lessons given by Catherine, an early childhood and elementary school science teacher in the midwestern US. Dividing his analysis into three overlapping and non-hierarchical parts (individual, social, and sociopolitical), he describes "genealogies" of her emotions; "how the trajectories of emotional experiences are positioned and position teachers to know and feel in certain ways" (p. 98). Zembylas's research, then, explores the interplay between emotions as experienced by an individual and as socially mandated within institutions. Guiding this interplay are what he calls "emotional rules" (p. 43), deeming what is acceptable or not in this educational context.

In his analysis of emotions on the individual plane Zembylas focuses on Catherine's reliance on her excitement as a guide to pedagogical decision-making. Based on classroom observations and Catherine's emotion diary Zembylas notes that excitement is the primary emotion driving her practice.[2] It is the emotional glue connecting her to the children she teaches, her belief in scientific inquiry, and her self-image as an engaged teacher. In addition, her excitement mingles with the children's in a contagious give-and-take, driving her decision-making within that emotional context.

At the social level, the flagging of excitement signals to her that something is not working in her pedagogy and a different approach is required. In one interesting excerpt from her emotion diary, she describes a lesson in which her initial excitement died down when she noticed a group of students going off task. Feeling both disappointed and irritated, Catherine tried to engage them, but then realized that their disengagement might have been due to their inability to carry out the assignment on their own. Awareness of her irritation guided her to ask herself whether, in fact, the parameters had been sufficiently clear and when she decided they had not, to work with the disengaged students on the task. Through their collaboration, Catherine discovered that they were able to go "beyond what we thought we could" (p. 104). Although Zemblyas doesn't analyze this incident as such, it seems to be a classic Vygotskian moment in which the teacher models and the students become engaged, going beyond what they were able to do on their own.

Most interesting and most relevant to the researcher's focus on emotions is that attention to her shifting emotions led the teacher to model and collaborate with her students in the first place, leading to greater engagement with the assignment.

At the sociopolitical level, Catherine grappled with the constraints related to her school's policies and conventions, especially regarding beliefs about how science should be taught. Included in this analysis are the emotional rules guiding which emotions were considered appropriate or not, in the teaching context. Catherine reported in interviews that at the start of her career she had clashed with administrators and other teachers over her desire to engage students in experiments rather than simply preparing them for standardized tests. Not only did she feel ostracized due to her passion for more student-centered curricula, but she desired different types of interactions with her colleagues than the ones they favored. Their talk focused on materials while Catherine wanted to talk about the emotional content of her teaching and the students' learning. However, her attempts to engage at the affective level were rebuffed, due mainly to the fact that other teachers regarded her methods as strange, especially her focus on "in-depth integrated investigations" (p. 107).

Despite an atmosphere in her school of preparing for tests, teaching "facts," and keeping emotions at bay, Catherine continued to be guided by her emotions, maintaining the emotion diary, in which she reflected on her and her students' emotions. Eventually she connected to a world beyond her school, reaching out to parents, attending conferences, working with university faculty in her town, and acting as a mentor to future teachers. These connections legitimized her emotions-based teaching approach, giving social support for what had previously been a private struggle. According to Zembylas, teacher education would benefit from greater attention to "the emotional and relational aspects of teaching" (p. 132). This requires acknowledging emotion as "constitutive of the activity of teaching" (p. 132) at the individual, interpersonal, and institutional levels. Above all, Zembylas calls for developing "emotional affinities" (p. 133) with peers as a way for teachers to collectively examine their private and social feelings and to organize for needed policy changes grounded in their emotions. I take up these concepts in Chapter 7.

Application of Critical Theories and Emotions/Affect to ELT

Returning to the questions with which I opened the chapter: What might be some benefits of attending to emotions? What areas of investigation are opened up? In answer to the first question, it seems to me that by connecting mind and body, attention to emotions offers several benefits: 1) a window onto moment-by-moment pedagogical decision-making guided by emotions, such as Zemblyas describes; 2) a finely-grained tool for attending to students' oral and written contributions, as in the Albrecht-Crane and Grey model; 3) a study of subjectivity that looks beyond static notions of identities to more fluid and embodied ones, as Kramsch (2009) discusses; and 4) theorizing critical praxis not with the aim of radical transformation, but rather as small and subtle shifts in perception or understanding that in themselves signal change and might cumulatively lead to further change, as Albrecht-Crane discusses.

In terms of methodology, in the next four chapters, I will apply critical/emotional theories to English language teaching in the following ways: 1) sticky objects in the classroom, as theorized by Ahmed, based on surveys of teachers and students, in Chapter 4; 2) micro-level analysis of the subtle dynamics of classroom discourse, based on students' writing and oral contributions, such as Albrecht-Crane and Grey discuss, in Chapter 5; 3) foreign and English language learners' embodied emotions related learning additional languages, as revealed by their metaphors, based on Kramsch's research, in Chapter 6; and 4) attention to teachers' emotion work based on interviews, such as those carried out by Zemblyas, in Chapter 7.

In the next part of the book, Praxis, I will weave all of these concerns and methods together to demonstrate how emotions might be applied to critical teaching. My aim is not to offer a template, but rather examples of the texture of classrooms in which teachers and students are engaged with emotions/affect along with other dimensions.

PART 2
Praxis

4
STICKY OBJECTS IN ELT CLASSROOMS
Hope/Disappointment; Resentment/Attachment

> Good and bad feelings accumulate "around" objects, such that those objects become sticky.
>
> (Ahmed, 2010, p 44)

> Emotions are intentional in the sense that they are "about" something: they involve a direction or orientation towards an object ... Emotions are both about objects, which they hence shape, and are also shaped by contact with other objects.
>
> (Ahmed, 2004a, p. 7)

This first chapter of the Praxis section of the book is devoted to a single notion proposed by Sara Ahmed in relation to the study of emotions: sticky objects. I begin with sticky objects because it is a refreshingly tangible way to discuss emotion and therefore a break from the abstract theories presented in chapters 2 and 3. This is not to say that sticky objects are untheorized. Rather they demonstrate elegantly a way to connect theory and practice, to carry out praxis in an intellectually-engaging yet concrete way.

According to Ahmed (2004a), emotions do not just move, but also attach. They are "what connects us to this or that" (p 11). Therefore, a way to examine emotions in English language teaching is to study objects to which emotions adhere, those that are particularly sticky. This exploration of sticky objects is a way to highlight the role of emotions, to bridge the gap between body and mind, affect and cognition, passion and reason. Examining stickiness could also potentially be helpful in addressing tensions and concerns related to teaching and learning, as well as notions about language that might affect acquisition and use.

Various sticky objects come to mind in the context of English language teaching, including writing assignments, teachers' written commentary about student writing, textbooks, tests, grades, and so on. Emotional responses to these objects are mediated by the degree of contact and types of experiences students and teachers have had with them: "stickiness depends on histories of contact that have already impressed upon the surface of the object" (Ahmed 2004a, p. 90). Despite the probability that teachers' and students' differing and sometimes conflicting emotional responses to classroom-based objects may affect teaching and learning, this aspect of pedagogy has not been examined in the ELT literature.

To redress that omission, this chapter explores teachers' and students' responses to particular objects that come into play in ELT. The two objects I chose to focus on have been particularly sticky in my own English language teaching: dictionaries and cellphones. I therefore assumed that other EL teachers, as well as the English language learners I teach, would offer interesting commentary when questioned about their emotional responses to them. To that end, I circulated two questionnaires to EL instructors within and outside my university, one about dictionary use in the classroom and the other about cellphone use (see Boxes 4.1 and 4.2).

I also distributed questionnaires about the same objects to English language learners in one of my classes, one at the start of the fall 2010 semester about dictionaries and two at the end, one about dictionaries and the other about cellphones.

The goal of this research was to answer the following questions: 1) Which emotions stick to these objects? 2) Do teachers and students have the same affective responses to them? If so, what are the common emotions? If not, what are the different emotions? 3) How can these findings inform ELT by deepening understanding of students' expectations regarding their learning? 4) What are the implications of these findings for critical teaching?

The results of the surveys are reported later in this chapter. However, first I will discuss Sara Ahmed's concept of sticky objects, including examples she and others offer. At the end of the chapter I offer suggestions for critical teaching based on the findings.

Examples of Sticky Objects

Feelings may stick to some objects, and slide over others.

(Ahmed, 2004a, p. 8)

In the Introduction to *The Cultural Politics of Emotion*, Ahmed (2004a) outlines her approach to emotions, one that examines "how emotions work to shape the 'surfaces' of individual and collective bodies" (p. 1). Conceptualizing "surfaces" is a way to theorize how bodies, objects, ideas, and institutions shape each other in proximity and through contact. In fact, a central question for Ahmed, "What sticks?" (p. 11), is a heuristic for examining objects and signs that may be oppressive, including her interest in "how power shapes the very surfaces of bodies as well as worlds" (p. 12).

A clear and dramatic example of Ahmed's notion of sticky objects, offered by archaeologist Harris (2010), is an urn containing the ashes of a cremated body.

According to Harris, the urn becomes sticky with affect as it engages mourners' connections between past, present, and future, revealing emotions "as a contextual property of things, one that emerges through the interactions and engagements they have with people" (p. 360).

Another compelling example of a sticky object, though not referred to as such, is Vandrick's (2009) discussion of her complicated relationship with teacups. In the chapter "Tea and TESOL," she takes readers through various emotions that stick to teacups, highlighting her ambivalence about her attraction to them. On the positive side of her ambivalence, teacups signify women around the world congregating to discuss their interests and concerns: "women leaning toward each other, in a buzz of eager voices, a community of women sharing their connections" (p. 36). Another positive association of teacups is their evocation of the mother–daughter relationship, one she has celebrated with her own daughter by going to teas at hotels in cities around the world.

Other positive emotions sticking to teacups for Vandrick are their association to her love of British literary novels and to happy memories of her life as a child of missionaries in India. There Vandrick grew used to having tea, a pleasurable ritual in her daily life: a "reassuring routine of our lives in this faraway but very familiar and comfortable place we lived" (p. 38). Yet another example of teacups as happy objects is their use in celebrations of friends' birthdays and accomplishments. In this example, Vandrick describes not just the stickiness of teacups, but also the way these objects stick to other objects:

> ... the exquisite teapots and teacups and the accompanying paraphernalia (tea strainer, silver teaspoons, china or silver creamer and sugar bowls, tea cozies), the fragrant black tea itself (often with names that evoke my childhood in India, such as Darjeeling, Assam, and Nilgiri), the descriptions of the tea on the elaborate, ornately scripted menu, the tiered tray with the dainty treats that accompany the tea (scones, crumpets, Devonshire cream, lemon curd, tiny cakes and shortbread ...).
>
> (p. 41)

However, while extolling the beauty of teacups and the comfort and happy associations they offer, Vandrick expresses her "discomfort" with them as a "symbol of a certain kind of privilege" (p. 43). One observation about their association with privilege is that partaking in a formal tea is a luxury, not required for nourishing the human body, and therefore indulged in only by those of higher social classes with time on their hands as well as financial resources. Another association Vandrick makes between teacups and privilege is that in the United States and other parts of the world, those who attend formal teas are by-and-large white, while the servers are mainly people of color. Social class privilege sticking to teacups can also be seen in the fact that workers on tea plantations, often women, are poorly paid and that they work in difficult physical conditions.

Most interesting in Vandrick's discussion of teacups is the tension between the injustice and comfort these objects evoke. This is a tension she does not attempt to resolve, but rather underscores, allowing it to remain stuck to these objects she desires and disdains. Although she takes pleasure in "simply and uncomplicatedly enjoy[ing] the steaming fragrant tea, the ceremony of drinking tea, the accoutrements, the beloved teacups ..." (p. 50), she nonetheless allows her awareness of privilege and injustice to permeate the experience. This conscious ambivalence makes teacups particularly sticky.

Ahmed's examples of sticky objects, on the other hand, are not mainly of tangible objects, but instead of words and concepts, including epithets, such as "Paki" and "international terrorist" (Ahmed 2004b) and social mandates, such as "happy family" (Ahmed 2010). Her analyses of these objects show not only how emotions stick to them, but also how they attract other objects and still other emotions.

For example, in discussing speeches made by William Hague, former leader of the British Conservative Party, about those seeking asylum in the UK, Ahmed explains how his use of the words "flood" and "swamped" attracted other words, such as "dirt" and "sewage," due to the fear they provoked and the "anxiety of being 'overwhelmed' by the actual or potential proximity of others" (p. 122). Even when Hague was criticized for using "swamped" in reference to humans and thereafter replaced it with "overwhelmed," his words still created "impressions" of asylum seekers invading "the space of the nation, threatening its existence" (p. 122).

Furthering her analysis of how stickiness operates, Ahmed goes back to earlier speeches made by Hague in which he distinguished "genuine" and "bogus" asylum seekers (p. 122). On the one hand, this distinction allows citizens to congratulate themselves for their generosity in opening up the country to "deserving" asylum seekers. On the other hand, the distinction justifies limiting hospitality, due to the specter of unworthy ones.[1] According to Ahmed, by constructing two types of asylum seekers, Hague sets up an ambiguity that provokes even greater anxiety: How can citizens ever be sure which asylum seekers are genuine and which are bogus? This uncertainty leads to further suspicion of all asylum seekers as potentially harmful to the "national body" (p. 122). Lack of clarity about worthiness renders them all as "figures of hate," thus intensifying stickiness "precisely because they do not have a fixed referent" (p. 123). The murkiness of who is worthy and who is not in this situation creates conditions for even more stickiness.

Moving to another example is Ahmed's (2010) analysis of the "happy family," an emotional magnet attracting other sticky objects, such as the wedding day, the family table, and family photos. These objects stick together both because of the promise of happiness they proffer and because of the social mandate to perpetuate the family: "The point of the family is to keep family the point" (p. 45). This mandate includes the requirement that the bride be happy on her wedding day: "the happiest day of your life" (p. 41). If she is unhappy, others will be unhappy by contagion, undermining her own and others' happy families.

The bride's unhappiness is an indication that she is pointed in the "wrong" direction and has to align herself with the "right," socially-mandated feelings, pointing toward the happy family. If she does not make that correction she is pointed toward disappointment, described by Ahmed as a happiness crisis, or a gap between an ideal and an actual event. The bride's disappointment might attract self-doubt, with the bride wondering why the wedding is not making her happy and whether something is therefore wrong with her. She might also experience anger toward the "the object that fails to deliver its promise" (p. 42); "'happy' objects can become 'unhappy' ones over time" (p. 44).

The concept of objects that fail to deliver their promise has direct relevance to this chapter, particularly to my findings about teachers' and students' responses to dictionaries. To capture those responses I've subtitled the next part of the chapter "hope/disappointment." Hope is the descriptor for the promise of vocabulary acquisition offered by dictionaries; disappointment is the descriptor for students' struggles when trying to use them for that purpose. Cellphones, on the other hand, attract other affective responses, ones I've described with the shorthand "resentment/attachment," a pairing I describe later in the chapter.

Before discussing my data, I'd like to add that I'm mindful that my choice of tangible objects, such as Harris's (2010) urn and Vandrick's (2009) teacups, departs from Ahmed's focus on more abstract words and concepts. Aside from her analysis of the turban as a sticky object in the film *Bend it like Beckham*, discussed in Chapter 3, most of her examples of sticky objects are of ideas and texts. In my case, I used dictionaries and cellphones as a starting point for researching emotions circulating in classrooms related to teaching and learning, much the way Vandrick's discussion of teacups branches out to social issues. I'm less interested in the objects per se than I am in exploring stickiness as a concept, and, in particular, why teachers and students pull these objects toward, or away from, themselves in ELT contexts. Studying the emotional content of this pulling toward and/or pushing away may offer insight into students' and teachers' feelings and ideas about English language teaching and learning, including impediments and supports.

Dictionaries as Sticky Objects: Hope/Disappointment

Students' Responses

> To be affected by something is to evaluate that thing. Evaluations are expressed in how bodies turn toward things ... To have our "likes" means certain things are gathered around us ... Those things we do not like we move away from.
>
> (Ahmed, 2010, pp. 23–24)

The obvious, but nonetheless powerful, draw of dictionaries in English language teaching and learning is that they promise to increase learners' vocabulary. Given that ELLs uniformly express a desire for a larger vocabulary, dictionaries would seem to be an irresistible resource. For many years I've taught ESL reading courses in which I require students to purchase a monolingual dictionary for learners of English. Yet, despite the fact that students tell me on the first day of the semester that they want to acquire a larger vocabulary in English, some don't buy the dictionary, some buy it yet don't bring it to class, and some bring it, but have to be cajoled into taking it out of their backpacks, or pockets if it's electronic, when the class encounters an unfamiliar word. I've therefore often wondered what it was about dictionaries that seemed to attract such ambivalence: wanting what they seem to offer yet demonstrating an unwillingness to engage with them.

To learn more about this apparent ambivalence, I distributed two questionnaires to students about dictionaries, one at the start of the fall 2010 semester and one at the end. Though the questions on the two weren't identical, both solicited a mix of factual and emotional information. For example, I asked students to list the dictionaries they owned on the first questionnaire and which they used on the second. The first questionnaire ended with the following question: How do you feel about your vocabulary in English? The second ended with: Overall, how do you feel about using a dictionary? Most important to me were the questions about dictionary use, such as these from the first questionnaire: Do you ever look up words in a dictionary? Why or why not? Overall, do you find dictionaries helpful or not helpful? Please explain why.

Those related to dictionary use from the second questionnaire were: Does the dictionary help you? Please explain how it does or doesn't help you. Are there any problems or difficulties with using a dictionary? If so, what are they?

Students offered the following responses to the question, Overall do you find dictionaries helpful or not helpful? on the first questionnaire distributed at the beginning of the semester (R = response):

> R1: It helps me to understand better because it has clear meaning of words.
>
> R2: Dictionaries is helpful because that made me know the words of meaning and spelling.
>
> R3: I think its very helpful because it gives us meaning and origin.
>
> R4: I think dictionary is helpful because it can help us to explain words' meaning and how do use these words in a sentence.
>
> R5: I think the dictionary is helpful for the ESL students. Because it help students to understand the meaning, the sentence, and so on. That helps to find the adj, v, adv, n.
>
> R6: Yes, I find them helpful because it gives vivid definitions or meaning of what a vocabulary is and its part of speech.
>
> R7: Dictionaries are helpful. It makes me understand the exact definition of any words so that I can be able to use the right word in the right place.

The above responses exemplify the hopeful aspect of dictionaries as objects offering definitions, spellings, etymology, and parts of speech. The promise of dictionaries is clear in these statements. However, two responses, while acknowledging the promise of dictionaries, nonetheless raised the following concerns:

> R8: I do find dictionaries helpful, but when you have limited time to read a passage you can lost time searching for words.
>
> R9: Yes, dictionaries is very helpful for me when I am using. But *I always get lazy to open the dictionary* (emphasis added).

Even more interesting is the following response which, like the second one above, mentions the student's purported laziness. Yet, unlike the writer of the first response, this student finds dictionaries unhelpful because of what she calls her laziness:

> R10: *No, because I am too lazy* so I just use other words that are similar (emphasis added).

What is noteworthy about the two "lazy" responses is that the first states that dictionaries are "helpful for me when I am using," but the second states that dictionaries are *not* helpful *because* the student is "too lazy." In terms of stickiness, one student seems to use dictionaries occasionally, or in Ahmed's parlance she sometimes turns her body toward the object. The other student, by contrast, turns her body away from the object, refusing to pull it toward her. What does this refusal mean and how does it relate to perceptions of laziness and to dictionaries as sticky objects?

During the whole-class discussion of their responses, I tried to explore these questions with students, probing what they meant when they referred to themselves as "lazy." My interest in their use of "lazy" was of particular concern because it belies their engagement in busy and complicated lives as young immigrants, including working, going to college, taking care of family members, and trying to manage the emotional complexity of it all. An object that might help them navigate this complexity would be welcome; one that turns out to add even greater complexity or stress might be best turned away from.

What emerged from our discussion was a shared concern about the time it takes to find words in the dictionary, to determine which definition is most fitting, and to apply the definition to the sentence in which the unknown word appeared. There was a sense that the dictionary was a time drain in their busy lives, one that often yielded little useful information considering the amount of time required. I should add that this sentiment was shared by many of the students, even those who had responded very positively about dictionaries in the questionnaire. Once there was an opening to discuss the difficulty of using a dictionary, many chimed in with similar concerns about the time issue.

This point was driven home further in the answers to the second questionnaire, administered after a semester of using dictionaries extensively in class to look up unfamiliar words, study parts of speech, and find examples of word use. The questions:

Are there any problems or difficulties with using a dictionary? If so, what are they? elicited the following responses:

> R11: Yes, some words can't be found.
> R12: Sometime in the meaning, I still find the words that I don't understand.
> R13: Sometimes there is a word has several meaning. It's hard to find out which meaning match this sentence.
> R14: Sometimes I cannot find a right definition.
> R15: Sometimes the definition of a word is not clear enough to understand the meaning of this word.
> R17: Maybe lazy, but no for sure. All I have to do is just typing.

This last response is notable for a couple of reasons. First it's another reference to laziness, despite the fact that this particular student always brought her monolingual electronic dictionary to class and used it regularly without prompting, often helping other students with definitions. Given that she was one of the top students in the class, her allusion to laziness surprised me.

During the class discussion of their answers, time again emerged as an issue of concern. Regarding the problem of coming across several definitions for an unfamiliar word, one student mentioned having to "spend time to find out which word fit the meaning." When I asked whether the student found the definition after spending time determining which one fit, he answered, "Usually."

In terms of stickiness, what I gathered from the two questionnaires and follow-up discussions with students was that dictionaries were assumed to be happy objects that could provide much-desired vocabulary. However, in actual use, they often disappointed because of the time it took to find a word, sort through the various definitions and find the fitting one. This left my students in an uncomfortable position, feeling as if they were pointed in the wrong direction if they didn't use dictionaries or if they used them only occasionally and with difficulty. The stickiness of dictionaries for these students was grounded in ambivalence: Dictionaries are good so I should use them. If I don't use them or if it takes time to search in them, I'm lazy. The fault was attributed to the "lazy" student rather than the dictionary itself or with the complexity and slipperiness of vocabulary. Ultimately, then, it seems that for this group of students, dictionaries are happy objects that become unhappy due to the anxiety they provoke about time, already a scarce commodity in their busy lives, and shame about not using them.

Teachers' Responses

The promise of dictionaries as happy objects was apparent in teachers' responses to a questionnaire on dictionary use in ESL teaching. It included questions about the benefits dictionaries offer, any difficulties associated with their use in teaching, and what type of dictionary these teachers required their students to purchase, if any.

> **Box 4.1 Questionnaire on Dictionary Use in English Language Teaching**
>
> 1. Do dictionaries play a role in your ESL teaching? If so, how are they used? If not, why do you choose not to use them?
> 2. If dictionaries play a role in your ESL teaching, what benefits do they offer?
> 3. What, if any, have been difficulties or problems associated with dictionary use in your ESL teaching?
> 4. If you require students to buy or use a dictionary in class or at home, which type do you prefer: electronic or paper; bilingual or monolingual? Please explain your preferences.

Some answers to the question about benefits of dictionaries in their teaching were:

> R18: Dictionaries can help students develop a love for the language and for language learning. For example, students can learn about the fascinating history of English words from etymological information in dictionaries.
>
> R19: When a student looks up a word in a dictionary, not only can he find out what it means in the text he is reading, but also he will see other definitions of the same word and how it is used in different situations.
>
> R20: Once students are familiar with the pronunciation symbols in their favorite dictionary, they can teach themselves how to pronounce and stress difficult words.
>
> R21: Students build vocabulary, learn to properly pronounce new words, and learn to use prefixes, suffixes, and roots to guess the meaning of unfamiliar words.
>
> R22: Overall, dictionaries are a great tool which can help students become more independent learners.
>
> R23: I really love the fact that they can see so many examples of how a word will have multiple forms (happy, happily, happiness), helps them get the hang of prefixes and suffixes, Latin roots, parts of speech ... all that stuff it takes so long to get clearer on if they just get it inductively.
>
> R24: ... to nurture the habit of learning of new words.

One non-native English speaking teacher (NNEST) described her own attachment to a particular dictionary, a happy object, a trusted companion ("my best friend"), that offered the following benefits when she was acquiring English:

> R25: When I was learning English at the age of 11 (a crash course really) I used a monolingual dictionary. I still remember it; it was a Webster's dictionary with a thesaurus and it became my best friend. I carried it everywhere for about a year. Having been a good writer in my native

language, I was frustrated that I couldn't come up with enough words to express myself. I still have that worn out copy somewhere in my mother's house.

Similarly, another NNEST expressed the hope that her students would come to embrace dictionaries as "loyal companions" as she had when acquiring English:

> R26: As an ESL learner, I have found the different dictionaries I have used over time to be my loyal companions in my language learning journey, and I like to believe that my students feel the same way about their dictionaries.

Despite teachers' upbeat appraisals and warm feelings expressed toward dictionaries in response to the question about benefits, they described similar difficulties to ones offered by my students when responding to the question about difficulties or problems associated with dictionary use, such as this one:

> R27: Fairly often, students could not find the words for which they were looking. Another difficulty is that sometimes a student finds more words in the definition of a new word that he first looks up. In order to understand the definition, he now has to look up more words. Moreover, students cannot always identify the correct definition to match the text that they are reading.

Another concern about dictionaries was raised by two non-native English speaking teachers (NNESTs) who discussed inconsistencies among phonological transcriptions in different monolingual English dictionaries for learners:

> R28: The dictionary also provides very useful phonological information – although pronunciation symbols vary slightly from publisher to publisher.
> R29: The greatest problem is idiosyncracy with respect to pronunciation symbols, instead of using the International Phonetic Alphabet (IPA), with which students are familiar from their textbooks and from dictionaries published overseas, US dictionaries usually have their own system of symbols. These differ from dictionary to dictionary and sometimes contradict IPA symbols … It's a mess and can be very confusing to students.

In addition, there were responses from teachers that focused concern not on the challenges presented by dictionaries themselves, but rather on students' use or non-use of them:

> R30: Students are sometimes reluctant to use a monolingual dictionary because it involves more effort.
> R31: Some students find locating a word in a dictionary very difficult and tiring.
> R32: They kind of hate hauling it around.

R33: Students don't bring them to class, no matter what the penalty for not doing so.

R34: Sometimes the students get hung up with phonetic symbols; they are impatient and don't read all the definitions. … spelling is a problem, also (a cliche but true).

Dictionaries, then, seemed to be sticky for both the teachers and students though in somewhat different ways. On the one hand, the English teachers I surveyed are attracted to dictionaries as happy objects offering valuable information about pronunciation, etymology, and usage, both for themselves and, potentially, for their students. They wish students would take advantage of the information and embrace dictionaries as happy objects that might help them acquire English.

The surveys indicated that dictionaries were indeed happy for those already oriented toward English as a source of pleasure, such as English teachers and students who are pointed in that direction. However, the students I surveyed, young immigrants with an often troubled relationship to English as an impediment to entering mainstream college courses and the workforce, demonstrated an ambivalent relationship to dictionaries as objects that promise, but do not easily deliver, vocabulary. Hopes for a quick entrée to English vocabulary were dashed when students were faced with a variety of definitions, more unfamiliar words to look up in those definitions, and difficulty locating a definition that would fit in a particular context. The disappointment and discouragement seem to lead to the behavior I have observed for years: not buying the assigned dictionary; leaving dictionaries at home; not taking them out of backpacks in class.

Dictionaries as Sticky Objects: Implications for Critical Teaching

Where might these findings about hope and disappointment lead pedagogically? What are some classroom applications of the discovery of these teachers' and students' differing orientations, the first group turned, for the most part, toward dictionaries as "social goods" (Ahmed 2010, p. 41) and the second group often turned away. What can be learned from the possibility that students might experience dictionary use as alienating, finding themselves "out of line with an affective community" (p. 41) because they "do not experience pleasure from proximity to objects that are attributed to being good" (ibid)?

One pedagogical intervention would be to conduct similar surveys in ELT contexts to discover what emotions stick to dictionaries. Discussion of these emotions might revolve around students' reluctance or eagerness to use dictionaries and why. In contexts where time was revealed to be a concern, as it was with my students, this issue could be acknowledged, including the frustration of having to spend it so lavishly in order to gain what may seem initially to be very little. Rather than just exhorting reluctant students to consult dictionaries, thereby risking further alienation, we might explore that reluctance with them. In this way, teachers turn themselves toward students, toward their ambivalence and struggle, thereby aligning themselves with students rather than with dictionaries.

Researching the stickiness of dictionaries with students might also be an opportunity to explore varying theories of language, particularly contrasts between cognitive (language-as-object) and more performative theories. By legitimizing students' concerns about dictionaries as unhappy objects, teachers make room for questions about where language "resides": Is it a code found in grammar books, dictionaries, and ELT textbooks? Is it a fixed and static object to be transferred from page to memory? Promoting dictionaries as happy objects would seem to uphold the notion of language-as-object. Allowing for questions about dictionaries opens the door to other theories, including language-as-performance, making room for the centrality of students' identities and emotions.

In addition, performative theories of language could be enacted in their relationship to dictionaries. One way would be to ask students to read the claims about dictionaries on websites and/or on dictionaries' covers and in front matter. They could be asked to interrogate those claims and to write their own ad copy or front matter based on their experiences as dictionary users. Another performance might be to ask students to roleplay scenes between dictionary sellers and users, or English language teachers and learners, devising and acting out scripts that enacted both the hope for, and disappointment with, these sticky objects.

Cellphones as Sticky Objects: Resentment/Attachment

> We move toward and away from objects through how we are affected by them.
> (Ahmed, 2010, p. 24)

Teachers' Responses

Both the questionnaire about dictionaries and the one about cellphone use were distributed to the same group of teachers. More responded to the cellphone survey, perhaps indicating that these objects were more sticky for these teachers.

Box 4.2 Questionnaire on Students' Cellphone Use in ESL Classrooms

1. How do you feel about students' use of cellphones during ESL class time?
2. How do you feel when students leave the ESL class to answer a cellphone call?
3. Do you have a policy regarding student use of cellphones in your ESL classes? If so, is this policy included in your syllabus? If not, how do you explain the policy?
4. If you have a policy regarding cellphone use during class time, how have you handled violations of this policy?

As expected, the questions elicited what seemed to be deeply-felt emotions, such as the following strong responses to the question: How do you feel about students' use of cellphones during ESL class time?

> R35: Hate, hate, hate it.
> R36: It makes me crazy!!! I use the terminology of the airlines: Anything with an on/off switch must be turned off when you enter this room.
> R37: It makes me feel outraged, angry, and disrespected.
> R38: On a purely personal level, I actually feel kind of unappreciated and hurt which probably says more problematic stuff about me than it does about cellphone usage, but there you are.
> R39: I am not adjusting well to the age of technology. When a cellphone rings because the student neglected to turn it off before entering the classroom (as stated on every syllabus), I become angry.
> R40: It indicates that students are not interested in learning and are easily distracted.
> R41: I hate it. It's a major distraction + students tend to use them for other purposes besides learning (such as email, texting, blogging, etc.).
> R42: I absolutely forbid cellphone use in my EAP and other classes because they are disruptive. I do not even allow them to have them on "vibrate." I try to teach them about classroom decorum, and cellphones do not have a place in the college classroom.
> R43: I am totally against it … it's a real detriment to the learning environment.

The above responses indicate that in a classroom setting these ESL teachers saw cellphones as unhappy objects, instruments of distraction, intrusion, and disrespect. These feelings were exacerbated for some when, despite a stated policy or repeated warnings, students continued to use their cellphones to send text messages:

> R44: I forbid it, but it happens anyway.
> R45: But even with my stern approach, there is lots of sneaky texting going on.
> R46: It's a constant battle. But I continue to hold my ground because I believe it is what is best for them and their education.

Some, while resenting the intrusion of phones, nonetheless grappled with their awareness of students' need to be connected to their families. In these responses, teachers expressed ambivalence rather than pure resentment, indicating awareness of students' complicated lives and responsibilities:

> R47: Oh god, I HATE it. I've tried humor, anger, cold silent stares … pretty much my entire emotional arsenal to discourage it, but so many of my classes are at night (working people with families at home) that I've never been able to bring myself to totally outlaw them. That said, I find them horribly disruptive and intrusive.

> R48: It's inappropriate, but a fact of life … it doesn't bother me because it could be an emergency.
>
> R49: I believe that students should not use cellphones during class time. One possible exception is students who have families with young children and need to use their cellphones for emergencies only (they can set their phones on vibration mode and leave the classroom to answer a call).
>
> R50: No cellphones allowed unless the student has a medical problem or the student's children have medical conditions.
>
> R51: I suggest that if there is a sensitive, etc. problem in their lives … put the phone on mute or vibrate … and go out and and answer it if absolutely necessary.
>
> R52: Today a young woman's mother called from the hospital and of course I told her it was not a problem.
>
> R53: Use of cellphones during class time is certainly distracting, especially if they are not silenced. However, emergencies do occur, and cellphones allow us to act on emergencies in a timely manner.
>
> R54: I understand that some students might have childcare problems, and in these cases, they might need to leave the room in cases of emergency.

Overall, then, for teachers the stickiness of cellphones in classrooms seemed to be due to ambivalence: resentment over their intrusion yet, in many cases, recognition that students might need to remain in touch with their families. In addition, the emotional toll of policing cellphone use, including enforcing their own policies, was evident in the following responses, a point I return to in the discussion of implications for instruction:

> R55: I can't and don't want to cross-examine them about whether they are going to the bathroom, making a call, just taking a break, etc.
>
> R56: This is not an easy policy to enforce. As I mentioned earlier, students have a compulsive need to check their cellphones constantly, as if they will miss something important. So in order to combat this, I have to stay on top of students.

Students' Responses

My students' responses were very similar to some of the teachers' in terms of expressing support for banning or regulating their use, as shown in these responses to the question: How do you feel about using cellphones during ESL class time?:

> R57: I think students should not use their cellphones during ESL class because ESL is very important class. Students should be responsible because we have to learn English during the class to pass the test.
>
> R58: I feel it will boring to other class mates and effect students to learn and listen to the teachers.

R59: It's not really good because can't concentrate on the study.
R60: I think it is bad because you can miss the important section the teacher is teaching.
R61: It really inappropriate.
R62: Phones will interrupt ESL students to concentrate to the professor.
R63: It's bad, it makes distractions to other student and also may interrupt the teacher.

Yet, as with some of the teachers, almost every student made allowances for emergencies:

R64: If it is not important and emergency, student should not answer it.
R65: I think it is ridiculous unless it is emergency call.
R66: It depends who's calling for example I know some person calling for fun I won't pick up.
R67: If it is emergency or something very important call, but other than that, I think it would disturb both teachers and students.
R68: Kind of disrespect to the teacher, but it depends on the importance of the phone call.

What emerged during the follow-up discussion with my students about their written responses on the cellphone questionnaire was a unanimous view about the need to stay connected to families, in part due to their status as the go-to person in matters requiring English. As one of my students explained during our follow-up discussion:

> If my family members calls, it's important to take the call. We are ESL students. My parents can't speak English. When they go to the government, we have to translate for them, even if we're in class.

This contribution encouraged other students to discuss their critical role in their families as the bridge people between their non-English-speaking relatives and themselves or as an important member offering other types of support. For example, one student explained that family members would not call for trivial reasons and, therefore, she needed to keep a line open to them: "They know we're in class so they wouldn't call us unless it was an emergency." This and other contributions to the class discussion highlighted the vigilance required to be both a student and a person on call in their families who might need to step in to offer assistance at a moment's notice.

My students' written and oral responses indicated, then, that cellphones were tethers maintaining their attachment to family. They expressed a reluctance to completely sever this connection and shut out the outside world, due to their roles as mediators between home and the worlds outside. Juggling these positions seemed to entail making on-the-spot assessments about the appropriateness of cellphone use in class, as demonstrated in their responses acknowledging the distraction of cellphones as well as the unthinkability of shutting them off entirely.

This is not to say that all cellphone use on the part of students is a legitimate response to family responsibilities or emergencies. Surely "sneaky texting" goes on, as one of my teacher respondents put it. However, the cellphone as connector to the family is an issue that might be discussed with students in formulating a classroom policy regarding their use.

What sticks to cellphones, then, for both the teachers and students I surveyed, is a range of emotions, including resentment, attachment, gratitude, loyalty, and a general ambivalence about their place in the classroom. These emotions seemed to be provoked by the special role cellphones play in breeching the wall separating the classroom and the world outside. This breech is the focus of implications for instruction discussed in the next section.

Cellphones as Sticky Objects: Implications for Critical Teaching

> We can loosen the bond between the object and the affect by recognizing the form of their bond.
>
> (Ahmed, 2010, p. 28)

As with dictionaries, it might be instructive to engage students in a discussion of cellphone use in the classroom to reveal the emotions sticking to them. One advantage of this type of discussion is that it would allow students to participate in making classroom policy surrounding cellphones rather than succumbing to and/or violating a teacher-made one. A survey and follow-up discussion might reveal students' ambivalence about this object, highlighting ways in which it is sticky for them, if at all.

Teachers who are conflicted or frustrated about policing cellphone use might also express their concerns and/or ambivalence about that positioning. This admission would help students become aware of how playing the phone-cop role interferes with the demands of teaching (in Chapter 7 I further discuss teachers' "emotion work" in classrooms). This is not to say that these revelations would end texting in the classroom, but they might alert students to teacher's various roles and possible conflicts among them. It is one more opening to discussing emotions and ways in which they stick to objects, roles, and positions. Looking at the same discussion from the perspective of affect might allow students to view teachers outside the teacher/student binary, discussed extensively in Chapter 5.

Another area of discussion might be how to reconcile the world of the classroom with the demands of the outside world. In other words, rather than focusing on the cellphone as a forbidden object, teachers might invite students to discuss what it takes to juggle their in-class and out-of-class lives, their responsibilities as students, and their other roles as workers and family members, with cell devices as the link between the various worlds they inhabit. In this way, teachers facilitate students' engagement with complexity and ambivalence, helping them come to terms with the various directions in which they are pulled on a daily basis.

Finally, cellphones can also serve to mediate instruction. This point was driven home by two teacher respondents who mentioned the merging of the two objects, that is, the cellphone *as* dictionary. One response raised this merging as a concern and the other as an opportunity:

> R70: The problem is, as I mentioned in the questionnaire on dictionaries, that some students use their phones as dictionaries, and it is hard to distinguish what they are doing when they are looking at or tapping on their Blackberries, etc. I suspect some texting goes on.
> R71: A student who had an IPhone dictionary app said it changed his life.

On the more celebratory side of the cellphone-as-instructional-resource issue, Meurant (2008) champions them in EFL instruction, describing an assignment in which his Korean students created video guides of their college campus. They took videos with their phones, uploaded them to the instructor's website, and posted comments about each others' contributions. In another example of cellphones as resources, Grey (2009), whose work is described in Chapter 3, asked her EAP business students at an Australian university to document difference on their campus, using cellphone cameras and other handheld devices, as a way of engaging in critical EAP where identities, and spaces between fixed identities, were displayed and interrogated.

For their part, Thornton and Houser (2005) used a strategy called "language on the move," emailing three short mini-lessons based on a new word each day to their Japanese EFL students' cellphones. The assumption of this strategy was that repeated exposure to a new word, at spaced intervals and in slightly different contexts, would maximize vocabulary acquisition. The results of their study indicated the success of language on the move, that is greater vocabulary acquisition, with the caveat that students did not often study the words at the time they received them on their phones, but instead, waited until their commuting time to read the messages.

Before carrying out their cellphone instruction Thornton and Houser (2005) polled their students to find out whether they had email access on their phones. Ninety-five percent of these Japanese students had web-enabled cellphones. Clearly, then, the cautionary side of the cell-phone-as-teaching-tool is the issue of the digital divide. In contexts in which students did not have cellphones with internet access, as is the case with some of my immigrant students, the types of assignments described by Meurant (2008) and Thornton and Houser (2005) could not be made.

Another issue to consider is compensation for the extra labor required to carry out the out-of-class pedagogy these authors propose. I wondered when reading about their studies who would do the extra work of uploading student-made videos or creating and emailing supplemental vocabulary lessons such as the ones these authors describe. With many ESL courses taught by part-time teachers who are paid per course, the compensation for the extra time would have to be accounted for, to avoid exploiting already overworked contingent teachers.

To summarize the findings on sticky objects, then, dictionaries and phones are both happy and unhappy, depending on who is using them, how they are used, and what they offer.

Conclusion: Implications for Critical Literacy

> When learning is no longer geographically tied to a desk, the school library, the book, or the teacher who demands "all eyes up front", then old-style transmission and surveillance pedagogy becomes less stable and less defensible but complementary to the out-of-school-pedagogies and practices in households, communities, and workplaces.
>
> (Luke, 2003, p. 398)

One of the most intriguing, though not surprising, findings of my research on sticky objects was that cellphones seemed to irritate the teachers I surveyed because they drew attention from the front of the room to handheld devices that hold such fascination. This shift of attention from teachers to the sticky object is a reminder that worlds outside classrooms may be more compelling to students and that cellphones can connect them synchronically to those worlds while we're trying to teach them.

It might, then, stand to reason that rather than demanding a steady diet of "all eyes up front," as Luke puts it, we sometimes engage students in exploring their fascination with these objects and the content they offer, through critical literacy. In terms of English language teaching for example, rather than lamenting, say, "alleged drops in lexico-grammatical standards" (Luke 2007, p. 52) attributed to new media, Luke urges engaging the collaborative learning potential of the linguistic changes brought about by handheld devices.

In terms of vocabulary acquisition this might mean having students examine how language and technology interact, leading to linguistic change. For example, Luke (2003) suggests having them explore:

> the grammar of emoticons, the mutation of nouns to verbs (*to e-mail.* ...), changes of acronyms to nouns (url ...), the creation of new words (*emoticons, hyperlink* ...), and investment of old words with new meanings (*browse, boot*).
>
> (p. 400)

Engaging with these changes might augment vocabulary learning from an exclusive focus on searching for definitions in a single context to an exploration of how language and society change in tandem, with these changes leading to new forms of literacy that could also be acknowledged. Reading, for example, is transmuting from "bookish horizontal left to right text chunking" (Luke 2007, p. 53) to vertical scanning of screens. What are the pedagogical implications and how can we engage students in considering them?

The consumption of dictionaries as commodities is another area of critical literacy. For example, students can compare the costs and features of electronic dictionaries, which range from 50–500 US dollars, the more expensive ones featuring audio components, color screens, and content from a variety of monolingual and bilingual dictionaries. Some questions with which to engage students in critical literacy regarding these economics factors are: What does it mean for people of greater means to have access to more words, definitions, features? What do these differences reveal about the digital divide with some having faster and more powerful devices than others? How useful are the various bells and whistles in terms of vocabulary acquisition? What are other ways in which language has been commodified and sold in the marketplace?

When choosing the two sticky objects to study for this chapter, I had not anticipated their convergence and was therefore surprised that the results pointed in that direction. I had simply chosen two of the stickiest objects I deal with in ESL reading classes on a regular basis. That they came together in a way pointing to opportunities for critical literacy was unexpected and welcome. Aside from finding that the objects were indeed sticky, and sometimes converge, there was confirmation that students' and teachers' emotions stick to them and that the teachers' emotions adhering to these objects affected their pedagogy. This is a finding I explore further in Chapter 7 on teachers' emotion work.

5

REVISITING PEDAGOGY ABOUT MILITARY RECRUITMENT

From Indignation to Friendship

> When pedagogy addresses students at the level of identity, social positions or ideology alone, the underlying affective forces risk taking over if they are not attended to. Identity-based pedagogies – locked in teacher/student, progressive/reactionary, peaceful and compassionate/war-like and brutal oppositions, without an affective dimension of friendship – risks provoking fears of annihilation.
>
> (Albrecht-Crane, 2005, p. 504)

> Listening, for each teacher, is an act of becoming where the teacher lets go of some aspect of her own individuality and at the same time opens up herself to new ways of seeing and being.
>
> (Davies et al., 2009, p. 131)

This chapter offers another example of ways in which shifting, complex, and contradictory emotions enter into teaching and learning, whether or not teachers and students are aware of them. To illustrate these complexities and contradictions, I revisit one of my earlier publications on critical teaching, in light of my more recent interest in emotions. Unlike the other chapters in the Praxis section this one focuses more on affect than emotions, using a Deleuzian framework.

The lessons I re-examine focus on the presence of military recruiters from 2004–6 on the college campus where I teach (Benesch 2010). The earlier publication was my contribution to a collection of ELT materials from different theoretical perspectives.[1] My chapter offered an example of materials grounded in critical theory and the following theoretical assumptions: situatedness, dialogue, praxis, hope, and reflexivity. Given the attention in the Harwood collection to theories driving practice and materials development, I devoted half the chapter to explaining these assumptions. The rest of that chapter is an exploration of a series of lessons in which my students discussed, read, and wrote about the presence of military recruiters on US college campuses.

The affective dimension of those lessons is taken up in this chapter because though emotions were implicit in the earlier account, it is worth examining them more explicitly. To do that I will reanalyze one part of the data, in Deleuzian terms, as an area of possibility or becoming, a moment of departure from institutional constraints and the classroom binary of teacher/student. The analysis is based on Albrecht-Crane and Stack's (2003) proposal for a pedagogy of affect and Albrecht-Crane's (2005) for a pedagogy of friendship, discussed next.

After the presentation of the literature on critical teaching from a Deleuzian perspective, I will offer the socio-historical background of my choice to introduce the topic of military recruitment in an ESL reading course in spring 2006. Then I will present the lessons in much the same way I discussed them in the Harwood collection. Next, I will revisit those lessons from the perspectives of affect and friendship in the classroom, a retrospective account of my own emotions/affect during those lessons as well as my students'.

Also included in this chapter is a story about a military recruiter who "crashed" a conference presentation I was making, titled "Critical praxis as materials development: Countering military recruitment on a US campus" (Benesch 2007b), leading to a variety of emotional responses. Finally, I discuss an encounter I had with a student I found reading counter-recruitment materials on my office door, one I discussed in the Harwood collection, but that I revisit here through the lenses of emotions and friendship. The chapter ends with implications for critical teaching, including how the lessons on military recruitment might have been carried out in more embodied ways.

Pedagogies of Affect

Albrecht-Crane and Stack (2003) engage with affect as a way to take bodies into account given their "capacity to affect and be affected" (Albrecht-Crane and Stack 2003, p. 192). Their interest in a "pedagogy of affect" (p. 191) centers on how to come to terms with what teachers and students do and feel in classrooms and how this pedagogy might link to worlds outside and to agency. Yet these authors make a point of excluding teachers' and students' identities as a category of attention because, in Deleuzian terms, they view identities as molar lines, rigid social structures that position humans into binary groups, such as woman/man, teacher/student, adult/child. Adhering to these identities, they argue, reduces possibilities for the unexpected in classrooms.

In place of molar lines, Albrecht-Crane and Stack propose creating conditions in classrooms for lines of flight, Deleuze's concept of "instantiations of desire" offering a possible "nexus of change" (p. 195). Bodies in the lines-of-flight concept are without organs; that is, not social organisms, but rather "the material of which existence is made" (p. 196), in Deleuzian terms. Detached from social structures, bodies without organs are areas of destabilization, possibility, and change.

Albrecht-Crane and Stack offer examples of lines of flight from Sylvia Ashton-Warner's pedagogy and from Stephen O'Connor's teaching of creative writing in a New York City public school. In these examples, lines of flight are "the intense breakouts of flows of desire in the classroom" uncontained by molar lines and connected to life outside the classroom. Desire, when not bottled up or repressed is a potential source of change, engaging teachers' and students' bodies. The authors offer two compelling metaphors for what transpires when desire is released: the seams of the classroom are burst and the classroom is torn to pieces.

The other perspective from which I carry out affective analysis in this chapter is Albrecht-Crane's proposal for pedagogy as friendship, discussed in Chapter 3, and which I explain briefly here. Like pedagogy of affect, pedagogical friendship is grounded in the Deleuzian notion of becoming, moving beyond binary identity positions to create possibilities. According to this notion, the space between teacher and student is a mediated territory "where new lines of thought open up" (p. 493).

This is not to say that Albrecht-Crane denies institutional structures with their hierarchical relationships, including teacher/student. Teachers evaluate and grade student work, shoring up institutional structures. Yet, within and between those structures there may be "in-between spaces of resonances and sensations in the teacher/student relation" (p. 494). A pedagogy of friendship acknowledges the more fixed identity positions while remaining open to the places where regulation is incomplete, porous, unstable, or flexible. These places or spaces are "disconnected from specific places and bodies" (p. 494). They are areas of play and the interplay of identity (fixed) and affect (becoming). I illustrate this interplay later in the chapter.

Socio-historical Background of the Military Recruitment Lessons

The 2004–2006 period was a time during which the US military intensified its recruitment efforts, given the increasing resistance of young people to joining the armed forces. Waning public support for the war in Iraq led to the adoption of three measures meant to widen the pool of new recruits. The first was an amendment to an existing law from 1995, the Solomon Amendment, that withheld federal funds from colleges barring military recruiters from their campuses. The 2005 amendment to the Solomon Amendment stated that military recruiters had to be given the same access to college campuses as other recruiters, such as those from private companies looking for future employees (www.law.georgetown.edu/solomon/solomon/html).

The second measure was a signing bonus of $2,000 per recruit offered to US Army National Guard recruiters (Washington Post, Mar. 12, 2006; A01). The third measure was a law, Executive Order 13269, allowing for fast-track citizenship for documented immigrants who enlisted in the US military, signed by President George W. Bush on July 3, 2002:

> Those persons serving honorably in active-duty status in the Armed Forces of the United States, during the period beginning on September 11, 2001, and

terminating on the date to be so designated, are eligible for naturalization in accordance with the statutory exception to the naturalization requirements … For the purpose of determining qualification for the exception from the usual requirements for naturalization, I designate as a period in which the Armed Forces of the United States were engaged in armed conflict with a hostile foreign force the period beginning on September 11, 2001. Such period will be deemed to terminate on a date designated by future Executive Order.

(www.fas.org/irp/offdocs/eo/eo-13269.htm)

I noticed the effects of these three measures when recruiters started showing up regularly on the campus where I teach in 2004. As their numbers grew and recruiters began wandering around the 200-acre campus rather than remaining in a single assigned location, the student center, I became concerned. I would say, retrospectively, that I was simultaneously offended, alarmed, and indignant. Having participated in anti-war demonstrations from the late 1960s to 2003, when I marched against the US invasion of Iraq (Benesch 2008), I was offended to see men in uniforms patrolling the campus. To my eyes, my campus was being militarized, representing a direct threat to my students, many of whom were documented immigrants who had not yet gained citizenship. This meant that they were the target population of Executive Order 13269 and therefore, to my mind, possibly susceptible to recruitment.

Lessons on Military Recruitment

Given the growing presence of military recruiters, I sought a way to discover whether any of my students had been approached and, if so, what had transpired. Were they intimidated, seduced, ambivalent? Did they have the necessary tools to evaluate recruiters' pitches, including whatever benefits were promised? Before deciding how to proceed, I gathered various materials that might potentially be used in a lesson on military recruitment, including glossy brochures from various armed forces and more rudimentary counter-recruitment materials produced by under-funded peace groups.

However, the point I made in the chapter I wrote for the Harwood collection is that the materials themselves were less important to me than the praxis. In fact the half title of my chapter, "Critical praxis as materials development" was meant to convey that the materials I happen to have chosen to introduce the topic were less significant than students' responses to them and the dialogue that ensued:

… my aim in this section is not to describe certain pro- or counter-recruitment materials. Rather, I will discuss how I introduced the topic, how students responded to it, and how I modified my teaching according to students' responses. That is, in critical teaching there is reciprocity between the materials and praxis, or, to put it another way, critical praxis can be seen *as* materials development.

(Benesch, 2010, p. 116)

Introducing the Topic

I introduced the topic of military recruitment on campus in an ESL reading class during the spring 2006 semester, by distributing a reading that debated the question: "Should colleges be allowed to bar military recruiters?" (*On Campus* 2005). It included two short essays, one arguing for and the other against barring recruiters. Though the debate format of the reading seemed to offer balance, the question itself was problematic for several reasons. First, the Solomon Amendment required colleges receiving any type of federal funding to permit military recruiters on campus; therefore, the question was moot. However, of greater concern was that the question naturalized the power of the military, positioning higher education as the weaker player needing permission to bar recruiters ("should colleges *be allowed*."). A stronger positioning would have been: Should colleges bar military recruiters from their campuses?

Another concern about this particular article was that the title of the essay articulating the "no" position in the debate – "Students must choose for themselves" – is an appealing proposition to young people. I therefore anticipated that most students would side with this position. The "yes" essay, on the other hand, was titled, "Campuses deserve the right to choose", a more abstract formulation requiring students to imagine what it might mean for a campus to make a choice.

Despite my reservations, however, I used the reading because I expected the dialogic process to engage students deeply with the question, no matter how flawed the materials might be. Even if the structure and wording of the article seemed slanted toward favoring the presence of military recruiters, the classroom discussion and subsequent readings might provide greater balance.

Before students read the article, I wrote the debate question "Should colleges be allowed to bar military recruiters?" on the chalkboard and asked students to argue one side of the issue or the other in a short in-class essay. Only nine out of 15 students turned in this initial writing. Of those nine, six said that colleges should not be allowed to bar recruiters; three said they should.

Students' Initial Written Responses

I have grouped six "no" answers according to three themes (R = response): 1) choosing for ourselves (R1, R2, R3); 2) recruiters provide useful information to students (R4, R5); and 3) protecting the country is our duty (R6).

The three responses with the theme *choosing for ourselves* express opposition to barring recruiters, based on the belief that students are equipped to make a decision about joining the military and do not, therefore, need to be shielded from encounters with recruiters. Though other "no" responses included variations on this theme, the following three responses made it their main focus. I have added italics to emphasize that focus:

> R1: No, I think they shouldn't bar the military recruiter because I think that *everybody have our own opinion about that*. So if somebody want to go to

> the military *this is his choice*. It doesn't mean that somebody push him to do that. Some people just want to work in a military. And if somebody doesn't, *nobody can make him to do that*. For example, I know that I don't want to go to the military and nobody can change my mind.
>
> R2: I think colleges should allow military recruiters because some of the students might be insecure about their career and maybe the information they provide will be useful for them, they will finally find what they want to do, while others can *just say "no" and stick with their believes and choices*. As example, is I went to the cafeteria and one of the military recruiters approached to me, he gave me his information, but he didn't convinced me, because that is not what I will like to do in the future.
>
> R3: No, because *students have their own mind, they are decide for themselves*. If they are not interesting, military recruiters can do nothing to them. Also we could get military information from these people. So I disagree with allows to bar military recruiters.

It is interesting to note that though R1, written by a young woman born in Poland, and R2, by a young woman born in Colombia, argue for allowing students to choose whether or not to join the military, both expressed strong convictions about not joining themselves in their responses. They would therefore most likely be impervious to recruiters' appeals. R3, on the other hand, does not state whether the writer, a young man born in China, would join the military. However, like the others, he too does not believe that recruiters persuade people who do not want to join the military to do so.

In addition, R3 includes an observation found in the response of the second group of "no" responses (recruiters provide useful information to students). This theme expresses the assumption that recruiters are no different from other job recruiters. Their role, according to this position, is to offer helpful information students might use in making a career choice. Not surprisingly, this is the argument made by supporters of the Solomon Amendment who claim that the military is equivalent to any company seeking employees and that it, like other employers, should therefore be permitted access to college students to distribute their information.

I note that though R4 focuses on information provided by recruiters in a general way, R5 goes beyond, expressing the opinion that the US military pays college tuition for students who enlist. This claim can be found in recruitment materials, belying the fact the goal is to sign up soldiers, not support students financially while they are earning degrees:

> R4: My opinion is college should allowed to military recruiters. In my view college *student can get more information about job, benefit program* that when they start military in college. For example, in the college students learn different opinion about job. They can *get idea from military recruiter*.

> R5: No, I disagree and college students should not be allowed to bar military recruiters. The college students still need to go to school, and they have a right to join the military or not. Many people said that *military gives benefits and offer students many things.* Like *the military pay money for college students, and they will pay the students if they join the military.* But I think that college students have their own decision to make a choice.

Finally, one "no" response agreed with others that "everyone has a right to make their own decision," but includes a new theme, "protecting the country is our duty":

> R6: No, the colleges should not be allowed to bar military recruiters. Because everyone should has a right to make their own decision. I think that *everyone should guard their own country which is duty.* The military recruiters are related our country or our community.

To summarize the "no" responses, five out of six stated that students should choose for themselves whether or not to join the military and that colleges should therefore not ban recruitment. However, as I will show next, this viewpoint was interrogated during the class discussion of the initial written responses. What informed that discussion was not so much what students had written, but, instead, a testimonial from a student about being approached by a recruiter on campus.

Before turning to that discussion, I will briefly summarize the three "yes" responses. In contrast to the "no" responses, they focus on possible effects on students of being recruited. The stance is more personal, as if the students were imagining themselves, or friends, being approached by recruiters whose seductive promises of benefits might prove difficult to resist:

> R7: Yes, because the *military recruiters will effect college students, destroy his education.* Most military *benefit are very interest to them.* Also his family will lose their children by the accident or war.
>
> R8: I think that colleges should be allowed to bar military recruiters because *we don't want other unknown people in our city colleges who want to talk for 30 minutes and take our time.* I think if people want to join the military they'll go to the military department and ask them about benefits and other information. Also, I think that they shouldn't tell young people to join the military. People are free and they don't want to be bother by others.
>
> R9: Yes, military recruiters should not be allowed in colleges. The amount of student willing to leave school and join the army is more than the students who are willing to stay. *Contracts, grants, benefits, and social status tempt the people to quit.* Army recruiters must be able *to explain their real reason* in these business.

As I will show next, the author of R9, Isaac, a young man born in Nigeria, was writing from his and his friends' experiences of being recruited.

Discussion of Initial Written Responses

After students had written their in-class responses to the debate question, I asked if anyone wanted to read or summarize what they had written. Isaac did not want to read. Instead, he wanted to speak about his recruitment experience. According to Isaac, he had been approached on campus by a recruiter who persisted, even after Isaac had expressed his lack of interest in the military. Rather than accepting Isaac's demurral, the recruiter continued talking to him for another 15 minutes, trying to change his mind. Isaac had felt cornered, unsure if he was permitted to simply walk away from this man wearing a military uniform.

The experience had upset Isaac because he thought he had been racially targeted. To test his hypothesis, I asked the class how many of them had been approached by a recruiter, either on campus, in high school, or by phone. As it turned out, only Isaac and Diana (R2), the young woman from Colombia, had been approached. We noted that none of the Russian or Polish students had been approached and of seven Chinese students, only one had been telephoned. She, however, had gone voluntarily to the military recruitment table at a high school job fair the year before and had offered contact information, a move she regretted after receiving numerous phone calls at home. One young Chinese man joked, "They know Chinese will fail boot camp." Despite the laughs his comment elicited, there seemed to be an uncomfortable awareness that Isaac's hypothesis was upheld, at least from this small sample. The only two students who had been approached on campus were of South American and African origins.

It may seem surprising that Isaac claims in his written response that more students are willing to leave school for the army than stay in school. However, his comment supports the observation that Nigerian-born students seemed to have been enlisting in disproportionate numbers. In addition, of five CUNY students killed in Iraq at that time, two were Nigerian-born.

To sum up the findings of the initial responses, most striking is that while the "no" responses express a view of military recruiters as a benign presence and a source of useful information, the "yes" responses described them as a possible threat. From a critical perspective, it might be said that the second group has conceptualized power, either explicitly or implicitly. They acknowledge the power of uniformed military people over them and would rather not have to deal with the intrusion, perhaps feeling ill-prepared to respond. This concern was raised during the following class period as part of a discussion of the homework assignment.

Follow-up Discussion

The homework was to write two response papers, one about the "yes" essay (colleges should be allowed to ban recruiters) and one about the "no" essay (colleges shouldn't be allowed to ban recruiters). The response papers consisted of a short summary, a question, a quote from the reading and a response to that quote, and definitions of unfamiliar words. In class, students met in groups to share their response papers, including their written reaction to quotes from the reading. They were to choose one question and one quote per group to write on the chalkboard and share their written reactions to that quote orally with the whole class.

The class discussion began by focusing on the following quote from the "no" essay: "As members of the academic community, we have a responsibility to educate our nation's youth by preparing them to effectively decide complex issues through civil debate." To launch the discussion of that quote, I asked the student who had written about it for homework to read her reaction:

> I could not agree more with this quote; my mother always tells me that she will not be with me forever, therefore the best she can do is provide me with the knowledge to conduct myself successfully in life. The same is true in this case, college's obligation is to prepare us for the real world, they don't need to defend us instead they need to teach us to defend ourselves.

Students mainly agreed with this proposition. Those who spoke up disagreed with barring recruiters because they felt infantilized by that proposition. Yet, they acknowledged needing tools for dealing directly with recruiters and for making the decision about whether or not to enlist.

Looking over what else students had written on the board I noticed this question: "What should students do if they are not interested in military, but recruiters keep talking about it?" This seemed to be a good focus for addressing the request to "teach us to defend ourselves." So, I asked what might be possible ways to deal with a recruiter who would not take no for an answer, but instead kept talking, as had happened to Isaac. The students came up with a variety of strategies, including telling the recruiter they were late for class or pretending they didn't understand English. Then I asked whether they would feel comfortable simply walking away without offering an excuse. Though at first they seemed dubious, they began to consider this as a possible response.

Because this was the first time I had worked with students on the topic of recruitment, I wasn't sure whether I should pursue related issues. Should I interrogate the power of the military, displayed in the uniform worn by recruiters? Should I distribute some counter-recruitment literature? Should I tell them about students from the university who had been killed in Iraq?

Rather than raising these issues, I decided to end the second class by sharing my opinion, one that had been changed by their responses. I told them that before discussing the issue with them I had been opposed to the presence of military recruiters on campus. However, after reading their responses and hearing their opinions, I began to consider the possibility that having recruiters on campus allowed for the type of discussions in which we had been engaged during the last two class periods.

Backtracking: From Indignation to Friendship

> Stretch – that might be a good short-hand for what has happened here: a becoming-teacher-student, creating an alternative space of learning, writing, and education.
>
> (Albrecht-Crane, 2005, p. 509)

One thing that strikes me in rereading my account of the lessons in the Harwood book is that a description of the emotions driving praxis is missing. This is not to say I wasn't reflexive about the pedagogy, including what to present, when to remain silent, and how to proceed. Rather, absent is how the following emotions (mine and the students') circulated in the classroom around the topic of military recruitment – indignation, condescension, fear, curiosity, resentment, pride, appreciation – and ways in which they guided praxis.

Perhaps most interesting to me is that in leaving out emotions, I neglected to underscore how the affective dimension interrupted the teacher/student binary in ways Albrecht-Crane and Stack (2003) and Albrecht-Crane (2005) describe. A point made by Albrecht-Crane (2005), one I discuss in Chapter 3, is that in cases where students may be more aligned with the status quo than the critical teacher who wants to interrogate it, friendship could be the medium through which this disjuncture might be played out. Friendship might prevent alienation, fixity, or even compliance, and clear the air for productive discussions of views or solutions that might not have been considered by either the teacher or students, encouraging lines of flight.

To backtrack to the emotion that triggered the lessons on military recruitment, indignation seems to have predominated initially. This was the primary emotion provoked in me by the presence of recruiters on campus, especially when learning that federal funds would be withheld if attempts were made to bar them. Indignation, then, was the trigger for the lessons, though I was careful to hide it from my students, not wanting to show my hand and risk pushing them toward opposing recruitment, the military, or the war, thereby short circuiting an open discussion. There was also the risk of provoking a backlash, moving them to a favorable position on military recruitment on campus. Thinking back on the lessons from the perspective of emotions, I now see this type of reserve as a form of friendship, sparing students from confronting emotional content before they have worked out how they themselves feel about a topic.

Alongside indignation was a desire to protect my students from the uniformed strangers who might persuade them to join the military, thus cutting off their education and possibly their young lives. However, looking back at what transpired, I am fairly certain that had I broadcast my indignation, it might have been perceived as condescension, a preservation of the teacher/student hierarchy by which teachers decide what is good for their students. By keeping my feelings private and structuring the lesson as a debate, students' opinions seemed to have been given openly; their experiences with recruiters emerged on their own, with no direct prompting from me. Also, there was no sense of having to adopt the correct position, either for or against recruitment on campus, because my views and feelings were hidden. This is an important point to underscore regarding emotions and critical ELT to counter the impression that what I am arguing for is an open display of emotions as part of praxis. To the contrary, teachers' awareness of their emotions does not necessarily mean overtly demonstrating them.

Turning to Albrecht-Crane's notion of "the dynamics of affectivity ... as a form of friendship" through which students and teachers "produce new modes of being together" (p. 492), I think in retrospect that dynamics of affect were circulating during those lessons though I had not conceptualized them in that way. Nor had I considered the pedagogy to be one of friendship, where "new lines of thought open up" (p. 493). Yet, I now believe that friendship allowed for moments of interrupted hierarchies and binaries, even if they were fleeting, such as Isaac's revelation of his upsetting experience with a recruiter on campus. More concretely, what transpired was that students taught me that barring recruiters was misguided and infantilizing and that, rather than advocating for their banishment, I should teach them how to respond when approached. We switched roles, with them teaching me what they needed to function in that context. I was the student, learning what was appropriate in this educational context.

What happened was unpredictable and unexpected, especially the response written on the board about the "college's obligation ... to teach us to defend ourselves" that became the focus of the second lesson. Brainstorming ways to respond to a recruiter was a line of flight that took off from that response as well as the earlier one from Isaac that seemed to have set the stage for subsequent responses. The unpredictable denouement of the lessons was a discussion of ways to manage the unfamiliar situation of being approached by a recruiter. Analyzing the response strictly from the point of view of identity might lead to the conclusion that I was being positioned as the sage mother whose role is to give advice to her children. Looking at it instead through the lenses of affect and friendship, I now conclude that the teacher/student binary had been unsettled, leading to a playful brainstorm of how to prepare for a potentially unpleasant and frightening experience, armed with awareness and strategies.

In reconsidering those lessons through the lens of friendship, I'm left with the desire for similar classroom encounters, ones that "shake up and mess with both a teacher's and a student's sense of identity and position" and are therefore, according to Albrecht-Crane, "crucial events of political intervention" (pp. 493–94). I look forward to future experiences in which my identity as teacher is "unworked" (p. 509), allowing teacher and students to learn from each other.

My Recruiter: Fear, Loathing, Pity, and Bewilderment in Honolulu

Before publishing the chapter in the Harwood book, I gave a talk on the military recruitment lessons at the 2007 International Society for Language Studies (ISLS) conference in Hawaii (Benesch 2007b). The session was in a basement room of the Hyatt Regency Hotel in Waikiki Beach; 20–25 people attended. About ten minutes into my talk, a burly young man walked in and sat down, crossing his arms across his well-developed chest. I was struck by his appearance because he looked out of place in this scholarly conference. Also his lateness drew attention to his body and demeanor. Once my talk was finished, I asked for questions and his hand shot up. He announced: "I'm a recruiter and of course we target immigrants. We target all kinds of people." He went on to defend the US invasion of Iraq, as a way of preserving the US way of life. He talked about walking on Waikiki Beach that morning and how the war allowed for that kind of individual freedom. "Look around this room," he instructed the audience, "this is what we're fighting for."

Initially the reaction was one of stunned silence. His remarks were so unexpected, so out of character in an academic conference, and so unconvincing. If "this" is what "we're" fighting for, why had the recruiter come to my session in the first place? If free exchange of ideas was the reason for the US invasion of Iraq, why was the presence of a military recruiter required in that room? He had not addressed the pedagogical content of my presentation, but, rather, seemed to be contesting my right to even engage students with questions about recruitment on campuses or to discuss my pedagogy with colleagues. Yet, he righteously claimed to have a better handle on why "we" were fighting than the academics in the room. Little by little participants began to respond to the recruiter by pointing out that the premise of critical pedagogy was to question the status quo rather than submit to it, and wasn't that a feature of democratic governance?

After the session, a few participants went up to the recruiter to ask him questions. One reported to me that he asked the recruiter, who wasn't wearing a conference badge, whether he had registered for the conference. When the recruiter skirted that issue, the same participant asked where he was from. The recruiter claimed to be with the National Security Agency, part of the US Intelligence community, located in Ft. Meade, Maryland. When asked how he happened to have come to this conference, the recruiter said that he traveled around the US going to conferences like this one. Over drinks that evening, we pondered that claim, wondering why the US government would spend tax dollars to send a man from Maryland to Hawaii to sit in on a presentation such as mine, if that was indeed the case. As it turned out, he showed up for one more presentation the next day, that one on peace education. Needless to say, his presence was one of the most discussed events of the conference.

I raise this event here because it offers another look at critical teaching and emotion: the risk critical teachers may take when engaging with political issues, especially during a time of war. The implicit warning I was given about treading in this area, while oddly flattering, was also somewhat intimidating, mainly due to its unexpectedness. In fact, even as I type these words I'm conscious of the possibility that they might be read by members of the military seeking to monitor anti-war activities. From the perspective of affect, I'm left with a contradictory set of emotions about that event: fear, loathing, pity, and bewilderment.

While I loathed the recruiter's superiors for sending him to spy on scholars, assuming that's what had transpired, I pitied the recruiter who showed up because his size, bravura, and dismissive attitude were so out of place in that setting. And just as I wondered how much my students' ethnicity came into play when being singled out for recruitment, I considered this recruiter's positionality: Hispanic, maybe working class and therefore possibly susceptible to recruitment himself. Finally I was bewildered, and left with the following questions: Were the armed forces so desperate to drum up support for the US occupation of Iraq that they were willing to send a recruiter to try to justify the war and the recruitment of immigrants to a handful of academics? Who makes these decisions and how pervasive is the monitoring? I leave these as questions and return to those about counter-recruitment materials and their place outside of classrooms but on a publicly funded college campus.

Pedagogy of Friendship: I'm a Counter-Recruiter

During the spring 2006 semester when the ESL reading class was working on military recruitment, I continued to collect counter-recruitment materials. Yet, I was unsure about how to present them to students without short circuiting open discussion of their varying views. On the other hand, I was not comfortable about withholding counter-recruitment information, especially because on-campus military recruitment was not regularly counter-balanced with recruitment toward other career paths.

I considered posting some counter-recruitment materials on my office door, but continued to hesitate about airing my views, especially while students were working on the topic in my ESL reading class. However, toward the end of the semester I saw a film, discussed next, that urged me to be more public about my views outside the classroom. The day after viewing the film, I posted a flier on my office door, *Ten Points to Consider Before You Sign a Military Enlistment Agreement*, published by the American Friends Service Committee, a Quaker organization (www.afsc.org/resources/documents/10pts-english.pdf). The points include: "Do not make a quick decision by enlisting the first time you see a recruiter or when you are upset."; "Take a witness with you when you speak with a recruiter," and so on.

The 2006 documentary, *Das Kurze Leben Des José Antonio Gutierrez* (The Short Life of José Antonio Gutierrez), tells the story of the first US soldier killed in Iraq, an immigrant from Guatemala. The director, Heidi Specogna, traces Gutierrez's life back to an impoverished childhood in the mountains of Guatemala, his life on the streets of Guatemala City as an orphan, and his eventual flight to the US, riding dangerously on top of trains that took him through Mexico to the US border and then to Los Angeles. Gutierrez was assigned a foster family, earned a high school degree, and briefly attended community college. He then joined the US Marines. After completing boot camp, Gutierrez was sent to Kuwait and then to Iraq where, on the first day of the US invasion, he was killed, apparently by "friendly fire."

Ten Points to Consider Before You Sign a Military Enlistment Agreement had been on my office door all summer. One day in the fall 2006 semester, when walking toward my office, I saw a young Hispanic man reading the list intently. As I approached the door, I introduced myself to the young man, he introduced himself to me, and I invited him into my office. I asked "Angel" (pseudonym) what had made him stop to read the list. He told me that he wanted to join the US Army, but was only 17 years old and needed his mother's permission. She was opposed. When I asked why his mother refused to sign the necessary papers, he told me that she always worried about him. Next I asked whether he was a student at the college. He was and, according to what he told me, in good standing. Then I asked why he wanted to join the military. He told me it had always been a dream. Yet, it became clear as we continued talking that he knew almost nothing about the war or what his life might be like once he joined.

Next I asked whether he had been recruited. As it turned out, he had been approached in high school by a recruiter who continued to pursue him on a regular basis, through phone calls and visits. It seemed from the way Angel spoke about his recruiter that he considered him a trusted friend. At that moment I decided to call myself a "counter-recruiter," a term I had not previously applied to myself. I told Angel that just as there are military recruiters who encourage young people to join the military, there are counter-recruiters who urge them to stay in college. The main difference, I told him, was that military recruiters can get signing bonuses for each recruit they enlist. This was news to Angel. Yes, I explained, your recruiter might be offered a bonus if you enlist. On the other hand, counter-recruiters receive no bonuses. I don't know you, I told him, so I'm not worried about you like your mother is. However, I think you should stay in school and get a degree, I said, because right now you seemed confused about what to do. I then referred him to the first item on the *Ten Points to Consider …* list:

> Do not make a quick decision by enlisting the first time you see a recruiter or when you are upset. A recruiter is a salesperson who will give only a positive, one-sided picture of life in the military. Don't make this important decision when you are depressed, hard up for work, confused, unsure about your future, or pressured by your family. This decision affects many years of your life; don't make it lightly.

Finally I gave Angel *The New Yorker's Guide to Military Recruitment,* (www.counterrecruitmentguide.org), a booklet published by an anti-war group, Friends of William Blake, containing advice for students who are being recruited. Angel was surprised that such materials existed. He inquired about the group and then, to my astonishment, asked how he could join it. Though I never saw Angel again and don't know whether or not he chose to join the US military or any other group, I had at least introduced him to materials that could help him make a more informed decision.

Looking back on this encounter with Angel, I can see it now as an example of pedagogy of friendship between one teacher and one student with no prior relationship. This meeting was less structured and planned than a classroom event, though I had posted the list that triggered our encounter on my office door. I also knew students read it because it was marked with pro-war graffiti, a form of talking back that I welcomed. However, I had not anticipated finding myself in the situation of talking to an unfamiliar student about the advice posted on my door regarding military recruitment. Yet, as our conversation unfolded it seemed to me that in this one-on-one situation, my role was to be the foil to his recruiter. After all, Angel was not writing pro-war messages on the list on my office door, but instead, reading it with absorption. And he seemed uncertain about his reasons for wanting to enlist. It may also be that my original impetus for posting the list in the first place, the heartbreaking documentary about the death in Iraq of a young man from South America, was also guiding my response to Angel.

Because Angel was not my student and because he had presented himself to me, I felt free to act according to my feelings. Telling him I was a counter-recruiter was a line of flight, unconstrained by prior acquaintance or by having to grade or evaluate him. It was an emotional response to an unexpected encounter, an opportunity for compassion on a small scale, with unpredictable and unknown results.

Critical ELT and Affect

> what, I wonder, would have happened if I had asked people to write down not what they were *thinking* but rather what they were *feeling*.
>
> (Ryden, 2003, p. 89)

> ... the first point of departure in analyzing text requires an embodied acknowledgment ... we need to acknowledge and work with the affective reaction and then elaborate from there.
>
> (Probyn, 2004, p. 29)

When I reflect on what I might have done differently in the lessons on military recruitment, I consider the wisdom of Ryden's and Probyn's advice to ask students to write what they feel about a topic rather than what they think, as a point of departure. Perhaps this modality would have been a more fruitful way for students to explore their reactions to military recruitment. By assigning a debate on the issue of recruiters on campus, I may have forced students to make a choice that left out more nuanced, felt, and embodied responses to the presence of recruiters. I could have asked, for example: "How do you feel about military recruiters on campus? Base your answer on seeing recruiters on campus, on your own experience of being recruited or on your friends' experiences."

Probyn (2004) and Misson and Morgan (2000) offer provocative ideas about how to explore embodiment in classrooms through the relationship between texts and affect. Their aim is to engage students' bodies by inviting visceral reaction to texts. Probyn asks students to respond to texts beyond cliches or quick judgments by attending to what she calls the "goosebump effect" (p. 29). This is the "moment when a text sets off a frisson of feelings, remembrances, thoughts, and the bodily actions that accompany them" (p. 29). Misson and Morgan (2000) explore an "embodied aesthetic" (p. 91), one that draws attention to and extends bodily responses to texts.

Misson and Morgan view embodied aesthetics as a reaction to neoliberal outcomes-based teaching, a functional approach to pedagogy that disregards the corporeal. In its place, they propose that English teachers help students notice their bodily reactions to texts and cultivate them in service of producing "specific selves who are able to do a certain kind of pleasure creation in and for themselves" (p. 99), a radical notion in this era of a priori learning goals and utilitarian outcomes assessment devoid of aesthetics, bodies, and pleasure.

To illustrate embodied aesthetic pedagogy, Misson and Morgan discuss a way to teach an article on proposed changes to the Workers' Compensation Act that appeared in an Australian newspaper. The article was accompanied by a graphic photograph of a thirteen-year-old boy's mutilated hand with all its fingers missing, the result of his hand being caught in a mincing machine while he was working in a butcher shop. The article included information about this case as an example of the controversies surrounding what might be appropriate compensation for the pain and suffering the boy experienced.

According to Misson and Morgan the article has great potential for embodied aesthetic pedagogy because of the photo's transgressive aspect. They believe that it might "stir in students a particular excitement" especially given its being "almost unacceptable" (p. 101) in an educational context thereby possibly producing "an extra frisson" (p. 101), interestingly a word Probyn uses too. The (hypothetical) pedagogy the authors describe includes first drawing attention to the photograph and eliciting comments and questions. Next the teacher might ask students to attend to the positioning of the boy's body in the photo, his inturned palm facing the readers' gaze. They then suggest that the teacher might place her own hand in that position, thus drawing attention to her body and by extension the students'. She would then read the text out loud and ask the students: "Who's to blame? Who's responsible for the boy? Who's going to pay his medical bills, his rehabilitation? What about his future work prospects? And can anything be done to make amends for the pain he's suffered? Should it?" (p. 102).

The lesson continues with students reading the article, mapping the various players on the chalkboard, and organizing themselves into groups to debate the various positions, thereby embodying the different players in the drama. In the end, the teacher roleplays the Finance Minister extending with one hand the full amount of workers' compensation and with the other taking back the amount that would be the difference if proposed changes were enacted. The lesson, the authors conclude, reinhabits the body as text, offering both aesthetic and political experiences.

Returning to my own pedagogy, it's interesting to consider ways that I might have initially engaged students' bodies and visceral reactions regarding military recruitment. One way would have been to have them examine visual materials, such as pictures of recruiters wearing military uniforms, televised recruitment advertisements, or war footage. Or I might have had them roleplay recruiters approaching students on campus and acting out the ensuing encounters. These activities would have responded to Probyn's (2004) concern that teachers sometimes avoid provoking affective bodily responses even when engaging topics that focus specifically on bodies, in this case the physical experience of being approached by a recruiter in a uniform or the hypothetical experience of being in the armed forces and participating in a war.

According to Probyn, by avoiding texts that produce visceral reactions, teachers "retreat from the experiential body" (p. 23), thereby forestalling what might be deeper and more interesting oral and written responses. She therefore calls for assigning texts that produce "a flash" (p. 33), frisson, or goosebumps, thus allowing bodies to be "set in motion through our teaching" (p. 35) with unpredictable results.

Because recruiters are no longer a presence on campus, there is no chance to introduce materials that would elicit more embodied responses to this particular issue. However, a relevant example from my current teaching is a text I assign about the health risks of working in a nail salon, *Mani-Pedis Go Green* (www.hyphenmagazine.com/magazine/issue-18-action/mani-pedis-go-green). The article graphically describes the ill effects of this type of work, ones that students react to viscerally. In fact, I could probably do more to provoke even stronger reactions, such as bringing nail polish to the classroom and letting its vapors be momentarily circulated and inhaled. Mainly, though, the article focuses on the opening of eco-friendly nail salons by workers whose family members had been sickened by inhaling toxic fumes in conventional salons. So, this is a reading that could potentially join bodies, affects, dissent, and agency, especially if students roleplayed various actors: salon owners, customers, workers, and so on.

I plan to assign texts and other media that avoid shutting out feelings and elicit only intellectual responses, discussed further in Chapter 6. This is in line with Kramsch's (2008) recommendation to make use of "other symbolic systems (e.g. visual, video, electronic, cinematic)" (p. 178) to make room for embodied responses. My goal would be to foreground affect, both in the Deleuzian sense of unstructured energy and possibility and in the feminist sense of emotions circulating and sticking to particular objects and notions.

I believe, having revisited the military recruitment lessons, that a pedagogy of friendship in critical ELT is a way to avoid the false-consciousness trap, positing teachers as more politically sophisticated and therefore more knowledgeable than students about which political positions they should take. This monologic attitude risks precluding dialogue by enforcing the binaries that Albrecht-Cranes warns against: teacher/student, progressive/reactionary, peaceful and compassionate/war-like and brutal. Attention to affect and friendship may be a way to avoid imposition and to unsettle those binaries, in the name of deeper embodied engagement.

6
THEORY BUILDING WITH LANGUAGE ACQUISITION STUDENTS

Metaphors of Embodied Emotions

> One way of enhancing [teachers'] mind engagement is to recognize the symbiotic relationship between theory, research, and practice and between professional, personal, and experiential knowledge.
>
> (Kumaravadivelu, 2003, p. 22)

> How do we document the subjective effects of language on the embodied perceptions, memories, and emotions of speakers?
>
> (Kramsch, 2009, p. 5)

Every couple of years I teach a psycholinguistics/language acquisition course, one in a sequence of undergraduate linguistics courses that also includes introduction to linguistics, phonetics and phonology, modern English grammar, language change, and sociology of language, the other course I teach in the sequence. My syllabus for the psycholinguistics course covers traditional topics, such as animal communication, language and the brain, first language acquisition, and various theories of second language acquisition. Yet, alongside discussion of mainstream theories, I invite students to draw on their experiences as language learners to interrogate received theories discussed or implied in the assigned readings, as a way to begin building their own. I ask them to consider "what constitutes a theory, who constructs a theory, and whose theory counts as theory" (Kumaravadivelu 2003, p. 18).

Many of the undergraduates enrolled on my linguistics courses plan to become teachers; therefore, my general aim in introducing theory building is to encourage their "ability and willingness to go beyond the professional theories" embedded in course readings and in school curricula they will encounter in the future, and to urge them to "conceive and construct their own" (ibid, p. 17). In the psycholinguistics class this includes engaging them in the following issues: 1) language acquisition theories, like all theories, are open to dispute and revision; 2) their experiences as learners are not simply private efforts, but possibly shared phenomena; and 3) their individual and shared experiences "count" and might therefore contribute to theory building.

The two theory-building assignments I describe in this chapter were designed to illustrate how introducing aspects of second language acquisition (SLA) that have mainly been ignored, in this case emotions, might contribute to theory. These assignments were meant to fulfill the overall aim of questioning received theories and reconceptualizing them in light of previously overlooked areas of exploration, especially those that students might be able to draw upon from their experience as learners of additional languages.

The two assignments, made in the psycholinguistics course in spring 2011, were inspired by Kramsch's (2009) research on the "subjective aspects" of SLA, including "embodied perceptions, memories, and emotions" (p. 5), discussed in Chapter 2. Before describing the two assignments that sought to get at these missing aspects of SLA theory, I will briefly discuss Kramsch's rationale for the research she carried out.

Kramsch's Challenge to Traditional SLA Theories

Kramch's research was guided by her opposition to the notion of second, or foreign, language learning as "an intellectual, disembodied exercise in problem-solving and strategic thinking" carried out inside learners' heads or between their heads and others' (p. 28). She questions why, regardless of the approach taken by SLA researchers, language learners are, for the most part, viewed as "talking heads that have to be taught from the neck up" (p. 28). So, for example, cognitive approaches posit language learning as "a kind of cognitive grafting of language on a pre-existing mind." For their part, sociocognitive approaches posit "social scaffolding for the development of mind." As to communicative approaches, they conceptualize language as "a communication tool for the achievement of social tasks" (p. 2). Therefore, according to Kramsch, despite the differences in these approaches, they share a notion of language as a "transparent and neutral tool" (p. 2) for thinking or interacting.

Kramsch, instead, advocates a concept of language not as a neutral medium, but rather as "a symbolic system that constructs the very reality it refers to and that acts upon the reality through the categories it imposes upon it" (p. 2). As a symbolic system, language elicits speakers' subjective responses: "emotions, memories, fantasies, projections, identifications" (p. 2). Her interest, therefore, is in presenting data demonstrating the interconnectedness of mind and body, emotions and thought: "the affective resonances in the bodies of speakers and hearers" (p. 2).

Bringing bodies and emotions to second language acquisition theory challenges the fetish in foreign language education of so-called native-like proficiency, itself a contested notion because it entails choosing a single variety to teach, and using predetermined benchmarks to assess proficiency. The goal of moving students toward a single target, however that target is determined, also imposes particular ways of teaching a foreign language, including teacher modeling and continuous testing to determine who has met prescribed standards and who hasn't. According to Kramsch, this myopic focus on native-like proficiency crowds out what might be a worthier goal: students freely exploring novel identities and behaviors that differ from their customary ones by using the foreign language in various unanticipated ways without concern for predetermined proficiency levels.

Once the mandate of native-like proficiency is lifted, interesting possibilities open up: "the pleasure that comes from transgressing the rules, from discovering unexpected meanings, from testing how much the language will allow us to get away with" (p. 205). These open-ended transgressive explorations, Kramsch believes, are particularly important for US adolescents, the population she focuses on, who may be self-conscious about their bodies and therefore seeking ways to break from the physical constraints of their native language. Whether studying an L2 allows them to escape from or reaffirm their native or heritage language, multilingualism is a way to engage with "various possibilities of the self in real or imagined encounters with others" (p. 15).

While Kramsch's primary concern is reconceptualizing foreign language education, my aim in making the two assignments I discuss next was more in line with Kumaravadivelu's interest in demystifying theory by inviting students to theorize from their learning experiences. These assignments offered a means of questioning linguistics dogma by positing current theories as incomplete and malleable, subject to interrogation not only by scholars, but also by students and other language users. In the rest of the chapter I will describe each assignment and analyze students' written responses.

Assignment 1: *Combination Platter* and *In-Between Days*

The first assignment was based on two films shown in class. One, *Combination Platter* (2005), is set for the most part in a Chinese restaurant that attracts a mainly white clientele though the restaurant is located in Flushing, Queens, a predominately Chinese neighborhood in New York City. When introducing the film to the class I gave a few reasons for showing it: 1) though the setting is familiar, the perspective is of the waiters and owners, and to a lesser degree the cooks and dishwashers, not the diners; 2) the film demonstrates how social issues, such as financial problems, immigration status, and workplace tensions, intersect with language acquisition; 3) as an independent film, its pace is slow, mirroring the tedium of everyday life and therefore reflective of the daily struggles and emotions of the main character, Robert, a waiter in the restaurant whose status as an undocumented immigrant is a constant source of anxiety. After explaining my reasons for showing the film, I asked my students to jot down a few observations while watching it.

The second film, *In-Between Days* (2007), revolves around a Korean teenage immigrant, Aimie, newly arrived in Toronto, whose days are spent with Tran, a more assimilated Korean immigrant. My reasons for choosing this film were to show ways in which immigration, gender, and age intersect with language acquisition. As a recent arrival, Aimie is disoriented, longing for her father in Korea, alienated from her mother with whom she lives, and hoping for a romantic relationship with Tran who treats her, for the most part, like a younger sister. The pace of *In-Between Days* is even slower and more repetitious than that of *Combination Platter*, capturing the main character's dreamy alienation and monotonous days. Before showing the film, I distributed the New York Times review to my students, striking for the number of emotion words it includes, as can be seen in this excerpt:

> There is nothing melodramatic about "In Between Days," apart from the quiet strain of intensified feeling that the main character, a Korean immigrant named Aimie (Jiseon Kim), brings to her own experience. You get the sense that if she did not allow herself small episodes of strong, disproportionate emotion, Aimie would vanish into adolescent ennui.
>
> Recently arrived from South Korea, Aimie does not seem to fit comfortably into either her own skin or the world she inhabits. She lives with her mother, who is absorbed in her own emotional difficulties, and she spends most of her time with Tran (Taegu Andy Kang), her best friend and the object of all her pent-up love and longing. He takes her companionship for granted and seems increasingly drawn to the fashionable, flirtatious, "Americanized" girls who barely acknowledge Aimie's existence.
>
> How she deals with this disappointment, and her more general alienation, might have been turned into either a fable of self-esteem or a cautionary tale of youth at risk. Instead, Ms. Kim uses rough, naturalistic cinematography and sound design to bring us into a state of remarkably intimate sympathy with her confused, inarticulate heroine.
>
> (http://movies.nytimes.com/movie/339991/In-Between-Days/overview07)

After showing both films, on different days, I distributed the following assignment guidelines:

> Write a three-paragraph essay about emotions in the two movies we watched most recently, *Combination Platter* and *In-Between Days*, and their possible relationship to second language acquisition:
>
> 1) List the emotions displayed by the main characters in the movies *Combination Platter* (Robert) and *In-Between Days* (Aimie); 2) Choose at least two of these emotions and discuss how they were demonstrated and/or expressed in each of the films. (You could focus on how the same emotions were displayed by both characters or on how different emotions seemed dominant in each of the characters' lives.) Try to give specific examples by describing particular scenes or interactions; 3) Write a paragraph explaining how you think these emotions might figure into a theory of second language acquisition by exploring their role in promoting or interfering with language learning. Conclude your essay by discussing whether you believe emotions play a role in SLA.

The 16 students who gave me permission to quote from their essays can be described as: two recent immigrants, one from China, the other from Albania; two first-generation immigrants who came to the US as children, one from China, the other from Russia; five second-generation bilinguals whose families use the following languages at home: Thai, Arabic, Spanish, and Chinese; and six native speakers of English who have studied foreign languages in school and continue to pursue them in college or in their daily lives. So, these are learners with a fair amount of language learning experience, good candidates for considering the issues the assignment addresses.

What struck me in going through the data was that, for the most part, students viewed emotions in complex ways, not as fixed states, but rather interconnected and moving, similar to feminist theorists' discussion of emotions, described in Chapter 3. The complexity of emotions is demonstrated in the four themes that emerged from the data, each one listed and illustrated by excerpts from the students' essays:

Theme 1: Individual Emotions are Complex, Associated with Varying Responses

R1: From my point of view, it seemed that the personal circumstances of these characters caused them to react to feelings of anxiety in different ways and to feelings of resignation in similar ways.

R2: Both of them seemed more than just friends, but both seemed confused because Aimie says they are just friends but seemed to develop feelings for him.

R3: The two emotions shared by the main characters in both films seemed to be fear and depression because both characters seem to have their own way of dealing with fear and have interesting ways of hiding their fears from those surrounding them. ... [F]ear is one of those words that can have more than one meaning according to the dictionary but in the real world or in films such ways of sending out a message to others could have more than one meaning or containing totally different meanings.

Theme 2: Emotions Interconnect, Shift, Conflict, and Chain

R4: Though Robert and Aimie each experience a wide variety of emotions, there are two which dominate their lives, as documented in these films: longing and alienation. For Aimie, these emotions *intermingle* [emphasis added]; her longing for Tran isolates her from English speakers and from her friends, while her longing for her father and family in Korea isolates her from her mother.

R5: Since humans are social creatures, the lack of social interactions because of emotional triggers causes *a cycle of chain reactions* [emphasis added] ... anxiety causing lack of interactions causing a struggle in second language acquisition leading to anxiety increasing and withdrawal from the social world.

R6: [W]hen Aimie is asked a question in her class, she freezes, silent, isolated by longing and disappointment and uncertainty. Her desire for a singular connection, one with a boy who provide a sense of comfort and familiarity (both linguistically and sentimentally), and her increasing loneliness limit her exposure to and desire for a new language.

Theme 3: Emotions and Social Issues/status are Interrelated

R7: He is in constant fear and anxiety due to his status as an illegal immigrant and his witnessing of other immigrants being arrested and thrown out of the country.

R8: He has stress in working a massive number of hours, the immigration police, getting his green card, not having his family there, Claire, and also not being able to communicate. ... She is also overwhelmed with anxiety about money, her mother's problems, and the relationship (or lack of) with Tran.

R9: Marriage to an American citizen being the only option helps drive him beyond his preferences and comfort zone to date an American woman which he would never do unless there is a much bigger picture in store. In Robert's case hope has a major impact on second language acquisition. Since he wants something from this American woman he is trying his hardest to communicate with her.

Theme 4: Emotions are Embodied

R10: I remember one shot in the film: *his hands shaking* [emphasis added] by holding the spoon when he is eating in the restaurant with his friend because he sees the staff from the immigration department arresting illegal immigrants.

R11: Viewers can sense, even from *the way she walks* [emphasis added], that she feels weighed down and hopeless.

R12: [S]he feels homesick while she writes to her dad and melancholy makes her letters even sadder. This is shown in *her monotone voice* [emphasis added] when reading the letters.

R13: Aimie got shy and embarrassed. She was *blushing* [emphasis added] and once again was hesitant to repeat what she had already said.

R14: She sleeps a lot in the movie because she wants to escape from the real world which she doesn't like.

Given that this was the first time I'd ever made an assignment asking students to speculate about the relationship between emotions and language acquisition as shown through films, I was pleased that they made such insightful connections and observations. Not only did they comment about the complexity and interrelatedness of emotions, but also how emotions were connected to the characters' social lives, not simply private states. Most surprising to me was how several students attended to ways that emotions are embodied, described through their attention to characters' hands, gait, voice, facial demeanor, and sleep habits. I return to embodied emotions further along in the chapter in my discussion of the second assignment.

As to the more abstract final question of the assignment, asking students to speculate about how "emotions might figure into a theory of second language acquisition by exploring the role of these emotions in promoting or interfering with language learning," I found that though the question does not elicit personal information, certain answers, cited next, were particularly astute in bringing together students' experience and theory. The writers of these responses drew powerfully on their lives as immigrants, children of immigrants, or, in one case, a student of two foreign languages, to explore ways to connect SLA theory and emotions. Their responses indicate that language learners' observations and insights can be a key resource in theory building.

In fact in R15, the student not only draws on his knowledge, as a first-generation immigrant, of the struggles to acquire L2 in the adopted country, but also moves beyond the assignment guidelines to suggest possible teaching strategies to address these struggles. There is a striking confidence in this undergraduate's writing, perhaps sparked by the invitation to speculate about something he knows firsthand:

> R15: … feelings of estrangement and alienation are key factors in such emotions as resignation and homesickness (or sadness and depression). Furthermore these feelings of alienation and resignation are the most common overarching feelings of immigrants. It is therefore that in order to keep the second language learner attentive, invested and motivated to learn the language, the classroom must make the learner feel that they are a part of the community that is the classroom. The classroom has to be an integrative and, perhaps, as both movies suggested, transformative experience … The absence of out of classroom relevance and sheer focus on grammar and language rules may cause the learner to lose interest because of the difficulties that feeling foreign can bring. The feelings are solely based on in-the-world social problems and general distance that is felt by not being able to communicate. To ensure the learner gets the most out of her learning experience the class might do well to have a focus on personal experience and to perhaps show the students that they are valued.

The next response was written by a recent immigrant from Albania whose more personal, even raw, language seems to capture her current situation as a college student writing in one of her additional languages. The rawness and immediacy come through, in part, from the shift from third person, in the first sentence, to first person plural and second person singular. It's also interesting to note the mention of an embodied emotion at the end of the response: "the grudge in your stomach":

R16: Emotions are responses to all situations. But what if we are asked to do so in a new language and in a new environment, how do emotions affect these situations? Insecurity, inferiority, melancholy, fear, intimidation seem to overwhelm us while trying to be like the others. Fitting in is the goal, but what are you to do with all these instinct emotions that are in your way? The more fear you have the more likely you are to be shy; the shyer you are the more intimidated you are and the more you are going to miss your old life. Learning a new language in these conditions is very hard. I guess that's why they call it the hard way. Emotions can define second language acquisition because they get in our way and don't let us enjoy the learning process. ... That's why we can even become indifferent sometimes to learning a new language. Our unconsciousness tells us we do not belong there, and our stimulus is spent without even knowing why. It's the same feeling you get when you are feeling sad and for a moment you get distracted and laugh at a joke, but the grudge in your stomach is still there without knowing why. That's what emotions can do to us. They can have power over us and unfortunately they can have power over language acquisition as well.

Another response capturing the rawness of emotion in SLA among immigrants was written by a student who had been in the US much longer, since early childhood, than the writer of the previous response. Yet, he seems to have firsthand knowledge of the frustration of learners who are misunderstood or cannot express what they want to say ("when things are not going their way"):

R17: Emotions figure into a theory of second language acquisition because we express ourselves through emotions. Emotions play a role in second language acquisition because our form in language is according to our feelings ... This issue can be seen in the United States because people can see emotions get the best of the immigrants. Sometimes when things are not going their way all of a sudden they have the desire to scream and curse with their accents in English. Emotions play a role because it could have an impact on the motivation factor.

Finally, one response foreshadowed the second assignment, described next, on metaphors for language learning. Here the writer, a first-generation immigrant, contrasts the familiarity of using L1 with the insecurity of using L2, described as treading water in a bigger ocean:

R18: It is no doubt that feelings of insecurity and inferiority can prohibit an individual from willing to express themselves verbally. To make matters even more intense, it is even harder to express feelings through a second language. When you are limited to speak due to a language barrier, it is only natural to regress and turn to your native language for security and familiarity. For Robert and Aimie, it was sticking to what they were used to rather than attempting to tread waters in a bigger ocean.

Before moving on to describing the second assignment, I note that films seem to be useful tools for building theory with students because they show interconnections between language, the body, feelings, memories, relationships, and thoughts. They also seem to elicit interesting connections between students' personal experiences as second language learners and their more general ideas about SLA.

Assignment 2: Metaphors for SLA

The second assignment came one week after the first and was based more directly on Kramsch's (2003; 2009) research on metaphors and foreign language learning. In fact, the assignment guidelines included the following quote from Kramsch (2009):

> SLA research has ... bypassed a large domain of what makes us human, namely the need to identify with another reality than the one that surrounds us ... Many adolescents find in a foreign language a new mode of expression that enables them to escape from the confines of their own grammar and culture. At an age when they are conscious of their bodies, they rebel against the limitations imposed on them by constraints of their social environment. ... When we talk about desire in language learning, we talk about exploring various possibilities of the self in real or imagined encounters with others.
>
> (pp. 14–15)

The Kramsch quote was followed by a research prompt she used to survey 953 undergraduate students at the University of California, Berkeley who had studied a range of foreign languages for one to three years. The goal of her survey was to elicit metaphors for foreign language acquisition, as a way to uncover "the embodied aspects of a cognitive self: emotions, feelings, memories" (p. 53). Kramsch's prompt was the one I used to elicit data from my students:

> How would you describe your experience learning a foreign language? Choose a phrase, an expression, or metaphor that best captures your experience learning to speak and write in this language. 1. Learning a language is like ... 2. Speaking this language is like. ... 3. Writing in this language is like ...

Whereas Kramsch (2003, 2009) collected 1,496 metaphors from her survey, my data were much more limited: 23 students and 69 metaphors. In addition, while Kramsch sorted and categorized the metaphors herself, I asked my students to write their metaphors on the chalkboard under the three categories (learning a language is like; speaking a language is like; writing a language is like). Then they met in groups, categorized the metaphors on the board, and came up with a name for each category. I told them not to be concerned about keeping the metaphors in the three groups separate because that might have been overly restrictive and distracting. In addition, my goal was to engage them in carrying out their own data analysis, not necessarily reaching any conclusions or generating findings about the differences between learning, speaking, reading, and writing an additional language.

To start them off with some models of possible categories, I included a few from Kramsch (2009) on their handout: challenging the body's physical limitations; escaping the limits of one's skin; experience of biological time; pain of repetition without being able to anticipate the future; and physical experience of embodied change. It was interesting to note when going through the data that aside from one group that modified one of Kramsch's categories (changing "challenging the body's physical limitations" to "challenging body's physical or mental limitations"), my students came up with their own categories:

Stepping outside of comfort zone
Rising to the challenge
Entering the unknown
Challenging body's physical or mental limitations
Being able to get comfortable
Feelings of being stuck and not being able to go beyond
Feelings of intimidation
Transcending
Acquiring an identity
Going Nowhere
Having some fun
Experiencing something you can't control
Feelings of insecurity and intimidation
Working against impossible odds
Moving toward something bigger
Acquiring a partially useful skill
Conforming to new community/moving beyond the everyday

What came across to me in reading the categories was a range of emotions, including frustration, transcendence, fear, and pleasure. To show the data analysis process in greater detail, I include next some of the metaphors students drew from in formulating the categories related to frustration (Feelings of being stuck and not being able to go beyond; Going Nowhere; Working against impossible odds; Experiencing something you can't control):

running in place
having ADHD
wading through molasses

swinging on monkey bars and getting stuck in the middle
picking up a cool new rock that doesn't do much
being on a boat in the middle of the ocean with no oars.

These metaphors are striking for their relationship to embodiment, supporting Kramsch's assertion that studying additional languages may increase awareness of the body and emotions. A few more examples of embodiment in my students' metaphors demonstrate these relationships even more starkly:

Speaking this language is like trying to find your car keys in a dark room.
Writing in this language is like trying to paint a picture with the wrong color paint.
Speaking this language is like drinking fountain soda. It is crisp, cool and delicious. At first you're ready to take a sip and explore the taste, but then it hits your throat and you're sort of stuck. Once it goes down, you're ready for another sip.
Speaking this language is like buttoning a shirt with stiff, numb fingers.
Speaking this language is like making faces.
Speaking this language is like being full before dessert.
Writing in this language is like trying to paint the equivalent of the Mona Lisa when you can't draw a stick figure.

Pleased that Kramsch's prompt had been a useful heuristic for students to relate emotions and language acquisition, to express particular embodied emotions, and to generate and analyze their own data, I decided to repeat the exercise with the 18 students in my ESL reading class, discussed next. Because these students were immigrants who had just entered college, failed the high-stakes reading test, enrolled in one or more non-credit language classes and were subject to retesting, I was interested to discover whether their metaphors would differ from the ones generated by the language acquisition students, who had been in college, and in most cases the US, longer and were generally more settled and secure.

English Language Learners' Metaphors

My overall impression of the English language learners' data is that it is similar to a subset of Kramsch's: those offered by students enrolled in the first two years of a foreign language. These metaphors "clustered around the physical duress and the skill-learning aspects of language acquisition" (p. 59), contrasting with those from students in Kramsch's survey who had studied foreign languages for a longer period of time. Their metaphors, by contrast, revolved around acquiring new identities, traveling, and creativity, as did some of my language acquisition students'.

Students surveyed by Kramsch who were at the lower levels, on the other hand, often described foreign language learning as a painful experience, dramatized through such metaphors as: "scaling a barbed-wire fence" (p. 60); "getting hit by a truck over and over again" (p. 62); "having a six-inch nail pounded into my head every morning at nine" (p. 62). These data suggest that learning a foreign language might have heightened students' corporeal awareness, by provoking "intimate encounter[s]" between their bodies and "new mode[s] of meaning-making" (p. 60).

To collect the ELL data, I reproduced Kramsch's prompt on a handout, leaving space for students to fill in their metaphors. After they were finished writing, I asked them to share with the whole class what they had written, encouraging students to elaborate beyond the metaphors themselves so that they could explain why they had written them and what they meant to them. It's important to add that students wrote their metaphors at the end of the semester, on the day they had received their scores after retaking the high-stakes university-wide reading test. Given that passing this test, along with a writing test, is a pre-requisite to the two-semester first-year writing course, itself a pre-requisite to general education and major's courses, the emotional temperature in the room that day was probably higher than normal.

Taking this context into account acknowledges that the metaphors students offer at any particular moment are contingent, not stable or fixed representations of unwavering concepts and beliefs (Kramsch 2003). For example, one student who passed the reading test wrote that learning English is like "winning the lottery," most likely a reflection of her delight at having beaten the odds by making it over the reading-test hurdle that day rather than her feeling about learning English on a daily basis. Another who found out that day that she had passed the reading test wrote that speaking English is like "finding a treasure because when people understand what I say, I feel I have found a treasure, I'm more confident, and I want to find more." By contrast, a student who did not pass the test wrote that learning English is like "walking in a big jungle. You feel scared. I don't have any idea what will happen and you are learning something scary, difficult, and challenge."

Learning English is like … /Speaking English is like. … /Writing English is Like …

Though Kramsch's (2003) prompt contains three parts, I have collapsed them into one, as I encouraged my language acquisition students to do, because I found no major differences in the metaphors elicited by the three, either in the psycholinguistics or reading class. In analyzing this data next, I will focus on one subset of my students' metaphors that seemed to fall under what Kramsch (2003) calls "metaphors of paradox" (p. 118). These are metaphors revealing ambivalence, contradiction, and "shifting mental spaces" (p. 118), ones Kramsch (2003) groups into categories such as: "contradictions between expectations and physical abilities"; "incompatibility of task and means"; "unpredictability of outcomes in time"; and "metamorphoses" (pp. 117–18). I find these descriptors of paradox particularly apt in capturing the interplay among frustration, longing, resignation, hope, and impatience in my data. Despite awareness of the challenges and sometimes pain of learning English, students express determination and fortitude.

In addition, there is an overall sense in these data of the physicality of language learning as an embodied activity, symbolized by cutting down trees, swimming, driving, shopping, cooking, walking, and so on, sometimes without clear reward or outcome. Yet, despite the lack of obvious payoff, students expressed the mandate to continue, to keep trying despite the odds. These expressions of perseverance were conveyed in the oral elaborations students offered when explaining their written metaphors, categorized next, with the oral elaborations italicized:

Metaphor of Paradox 1: Incompatibility of Task and Means

- Using a small knife to cut down trees. *It's hard, but you have to keep trying. You have to keep going. You can do it, but you have to spend a lot of time.*
- Swimming in a pool without a lifesaver. *I can't swim. If I try I have to put on a lifesaver. If not, I can't swim. Sometimes I try so hard to speak. It makes no sense to others, but if you keep trying, you'll learn to speak great.*
- Driving a car without oil. *It will stop. You have to keep practice. If not, you will stop in the same place.*
- Shopping without money. *When you go shopping, you see clothes you want. Like an essay. You want to write it, but you can't. Sometimes too much detail. You don't have the main idea.*
- Trying to cook food without experience. *I want the food to be good, but I don't have a lot of experience.*

Metaphor of Paradox 2: Unpredictability of Outcomes in Time

- Peeling an onion; it's endless. *There's no end to learning English.*
- Walking in the sky. *The sky is so big. It's like English, endless. We have to go step by step.*
- Opening a lock with a roomful of keys. *You have to try them one by one. If you keep trying, you will get it one day.*

Metaphor of Paradox 3: Metamorphoses

- Wearing high heels. *I can't wear them. I'm used to wearing sneakers. When I have to go to a wedding, I put them on in the house and walk around so I can get used to them.*
- Becoming Americanized. *I can't believe that I still can't write English much better. So when I write English I feel Americanized.*
- Adding sugar to water. *At one point the sugar won't dissolve. That's when you know English. So you have to keep trying enough to change the mass.*

Metaphor of Paradox 4: Contradiction between Experiences and Physical Abilities

- An old man crossing the street slowly and carefully. *I write a sentence that I check a few times and go on to the next sentence.*

- A fish trying to fly in the sky. *I can swim in the water (speak Chinese), but I have to fly in the sky to speak English. The fish has to practice his muscles.*
- A fish living without water.

These metaphors of paradox "embrace in the same field of vision two contradictory principles" (p. 121), thereby offering a chance for students to express the frustration and even the absurdity of trying to learn English as young adult immigrants with dauntingly busy lives combining work, college, and family responsibilities. Though reading the metaphors may suggest that this was a depressing exercise revealing language learning as a burden, the opposite was true. Students seemed to take pleasure in writing and sharing their metaphors, at times dramatizing the impossibility of juggling all the aspects of their challenging lives.

During the class discussion of what they had written, students were playful, humorous, thoughtful and, at times, ironic. For example, the student who wrote that learning English is like a fish living without water explained, with an ironic smile on her face: "They will be busy and struggle and it's painful and in the end they die." Another smilingly and touchingly expressed the delicate dance he does when speaking English as "showing love to a girl you love. You're nervous, you have to practice what you'll say, check the emotion of the girl, like happy or sad." Another surprised the class with her thoughtful metaphor about writing in English as "explaining the sun to a man who's never seen it. You tell him it's red, it's hot, it's a circle, but you can't really explain what it is."

Given what I witnessed during students' reporting of their metaphors to the whole class, I think it's appropriate to see metaphor writing and sharing as performances rather than indicators of core beliefs and guiding priniciples. Students fed off each others' contributions, adding to their own, and, in some cases, offering playful metaphors which they shared laughingly, eliciting giggles, such as, "Speaking English is like asking a dog to speak Chinese because some dogs speak their owner's speak. It's hard to get them to speak" and "Speaking English is like going to McDonald's and ordering fried rice. It's almost impossible because they don't have fried rice. It's almost impossible to understand every word." These metaphors were greeted with approval of their authors' creativity.

This is not to say that the more absurd metaphors were merely jokes. They seemed to be generated with serious intent and to reflect aspects of students' experiences. However, as Kramsch cautions, the feelings expressed in students' metaphors should not be considered reflections of "stable individual attitudes and beliefs" (p. 116), thus raising alarm when students symbolically express physical pain, or emotional turmoil. It might be more useful to consider them, instead, as the expression of "a belief space, that is in part shared and shaped by others, and in which various possible scenarios are acted out" (ibid). This understanding of metaphors as shared areas of possibility makes room for interesting classroom discussions about how students conceptualize language learning and how those concepts might affect their learning at any given moment.

With the notion in mind of metaphors for language learning as shared belief spaces and possible scenarios, I plan to repeat the exercise in other classes, starting at the beginning of a semester rather than the end. Engaging students in discussions about their metaphors will be a chance to explore the following issues: how beliefs are mediated by language; how beliefs are shifting, not static; how beliefs about language are often embodied. Exploration of these issues might increase awareness that language learning engages mind and body: emotions, memories, beliefs, and fantasies. This awareness might allow students to relate more comfortably to language as not outside them, but as embodied, performative, and plastic, a welcome counterdiscourse to the banal testing and quantifying of language to which they are subjected on a regular basis.

Conclusion

Asking language acquisition students to consider the relationship between SLA and emotions seems to have demonstrated to those students that theories are incomplete because they may disregard important phenomenon and that they can change when previously overlooked phenomena are incorporated. Evidence of the success of the emotions assignments in imparting these concepts came in students' written feedback at the end of the semester. Responding to one question on the feedback form, What was the most important thing you learned?, students offered the following responses:

> R1: I learned that perhaps there is truth to more than one concept/theory in regards to language acquisition.
> R2: Speaking generally, the exposure I received to social theories of language was most important to me; I want to learn about as many ideas as possible so that I may have the freedom to choose from among them and form my own.
> R3: The most important thing I learned is that despite the enormous amount of literature out there on practically every subject, no one seems to have a definitive answer for anything! Research seems to be a never-ending process, especially since things are always changing, including people's perceptions. Even when data appear to objectively show one thing, those people analyzing it seem to interpret it however they want to in order to fit their beliefs or contradict someone else's.

Though this feedback was very gratifying, I would not necessarily repeat the assignments identically. I might instead, for example, ask them to watch those films, or others, and to write about what they noticed in the films about SLA that is missing from the theories we had read about. This more open-ended question might lead to speculation about aspects of language acquisition, other than emotions, that theories have overlooked.

Yet, even if I made more open-ended assignments, I would still want to incorporate the use of metaphors in theory building with students, as vehicles for honoring embodiment, ambivalence, contradiction, paradox, challenge, struggle, complexity, and finesse in language acquisition. I would continue to ask students to engage with metaphors in both language acquisition and ESL classes to explore possibilities for awareness and critical distance.

Starting the metaphors exercise earlier in the semester with English language learners might also allow me to make greater use of the three triggers in the prompt and perhaps substituting "Reading in English is like ..." for the more general "Learning in English is like ... ." In this way, I might encourage deeper thinking about differences between speaking, writing, and reading, both emotionally and physically, to raise awareness of what students call upon when engaging in them separately. These metaphoric explorations would offer an alternative to a cognitive view of language that posits acquisition as solely from the "neck up" (Kramsch 2009, p. 28), one that underlies the regime of testing and tracking favored by educational institutions.

I end the chapter with feedback from one of the students in the language acquisition class because I think it demonstrates possibilities opened up when invitations to explore emotions in language acquisition classes are made. This student, a native speaker of English, was finishing up his undergraduate degree in linguistics and had therefore already completed several other linguistics courses including one with me the previous semester. His comment suggests that working on emotions explicitly as part of linguistics curricula may raise the profile of multilingual students, those often marginalized in US universities, such as the one in which I teach despite the fact that over half the student population was born outside the US:

> R4: I learned that the majority of people in this class were bilingual which was extremely surprising and gave excellent perspective in class discussion.

Emotions, then, seem to be an important area not only for theory building, but also for inviting contributions from diasporic students whose experiences offer a dimension that is often missing in the SLA literature: the messy, heartbreaking, exhilarating process of migrating to other countries and acquiring additional languages and identities.

7
ENGLISH LANGUAGE TEACHERS' EMOTION WORK

Management, Embodiment, and Explicit Teaching

> [W]hat the working day produces and reproduces as its primary and most valuable product is an affective relation to the world, to oneself and to others.
> (Worsham, 1998, p. 219)

> Emotion work refers ... to the act of evoking or shaping as well as suppressing feeling.
> (Hochschild, 2003, p. 95)

"Emotion work" was first proposed by sociologist Arlie Hochschild in 1979 as a way to theorize the role of emotions in the workplace, particularly in jobs carried out mainly by women. Her use of the terms *emotion work*, *emotional labor*, and *emotion management* acknowledged that jobs make not only physical and cognitive demands, but also emotional ones that are socially-mediated. Hochschild's (1983) often-cited example is that of airline attendants who are trained to maintain a constant smile and calm demeanor to reassure passengers. This type of emotion work, Hochschild claimed, can be more daunting than pushing metal carts and remembering safety measures.

My interest in English language teachers' emotion work is situated in a particular sociopolitical context: decreased funding for the public sector in the US and throughout the world, driven by neoliberal, or free-market, ideology. Two scenarios that play out as a result of diminished public financing are greater competition for limited resources and intensified privatization and commodification of various sectors of society that were previously benefactors of public funding or free (Chun 2009). In publicly funded postsecondary educational institutions, such as the one in which I teach, the do-with-less scenario has led to increased class size, greater reliance on contingent labor, and cuts in classes that serve disfavored populations, including English language learners (ELLs).

At the level of admissions to higher education, preference is given to transfer students who have completed their basic requirements at other institutions, including first-year writing courses, and can therefore enroll directly in courses for their majors. These students represent a smaller financial burden on cash-strapped colleges than English language learners and developmental writers who, because of the additional expense of offering reading and writing classes, are considered too expensive and more expendable. In addition, once students exit literacy courses they may require tutoring to help them with course assignments, an additional expense at a time of diminished funds.

In this political climate, reading and writing assessment tests take on even greater significance as gates to the mainstream. Therefore, ELLs may feel more pressure to pass them quickly and find seats in first-year writing courses where cuts are often made. English language teachers may in turn feel responsible for helping students pass reading and writing tests in as little time as possible so that students may continue their education and not get discouraged by repeated failure to the point of dropping out at the very start of their college experience. In addition, teachers may feel that their job performance is being measured in part by the number of their students who pass the tests, adding to pressure on them at a time when ESL sections are being cut and and class sizes increased.

With these conditions as the backdrop, I wanted to explore English language teachers' emotions, in particular the types of emotion work they carry out that is, for the most part, unacknowledged in the ELT literature and in their workplaces. Although I am aware that academics around the world have contested the neoliberal agenda of the "corporatizing university" (Starfield 2004, p. 138) with its demands for accountability, and positioning of teachers as conduits for delivering commodified knowledge, I wondered how defunding of public higher education and the concomitant pressures on students and teachers might play out in the affective life of ELT classes. If, as Holborow (2006) claims, neoliberal ideology "degrades human experience by reducing it to the cash nexus" (p. 97), leading to "smoldering levels of resentment" (p. 98), what evidence might there be of neoliberalism's reach in daily classroom exchanges, as reported by English language teachers?

This is not to say that I was seeking a cause and effect relationship between neoliberal ideology and teachers' emotions. Rather, I wanted to interview teachers about their emotions in an open-ended way without ignoring the sociopolitical context. While analyzing the data I remained alert to unexpected and surprising findings, using the lens of emotion work, defined more fully in the next section.

To collect the data I interviewed eight English language teachers from my university and one from a privately-funded US university. I located these teachers through local list-serves. Only one of those who volunteered to be interviewed self-identifies as a critical teacher and I was not particularly seeking teachers in that category. Seven interviewees were women; two were men. Five are full-time English language teachers and four are part-time. One is a non-native speaker of English while the rest are native speakers, one Canadian-born and the rest US-born. All are experienced EL teachers, none with less than ten years of teaching experience. The interviews were conducted between 2009 and 2011 using a combined form of Zembylas's (2005) list of teacher emotions (p. 220) and sample questions from his Meta-Emotion Questionnaire (p. 223).

Box 7.1 Meta-emotion Interview Questions for English Language Teachers (adopted from Zembylas 2005)

1. Which of these emotions do you feel most commonly when teaching:

Happiness/joy	Frustration
Sadness/grief	Disappointment
Anger/irritation	Disillusion
Fear/anxiety	Guilt
Disgust	Despair
Fascination	Caring
Pride	Love
Wonder	Intimacy
Enthusiasm	Loss
Boredom	Powerlessness
Awe	Compassion

   The following questions will be repeated for each emotion identified by the respondent in question 1:

2. What are your reactions to being (name of emotion)? What do these reactions have to do with your ESL teaching?
3. Does the way you feel about (name of emotion) have a history in your teaching career?
4. Can you tell if your students feel (name of emotion)? How? What do you do when a student feels (name of emotion)? What are you trying to teach your student about (name of emotion)?
5. Are there things you do regularly during your teaching to make sure you feel (name of emotion)? Are there things you do regularly during your teaching to make sure you *don't* feel (name of emotion)?

Each interview took one to two hours and consisted of instructions to choose from among the 22 emotions listed the ones the interviewee felt most commonly when teaching. This was followed by my posing the four interview questions listed in Box 7.1 about the three dominant emotions the interviewee had selected.

What emerged from the interviews was that these teachers do indeed carry out emotion work and that they spoke eagerly and easily about it, often commenting about how surprised they were that emotions were such a dominant feature of their teaching, something they had not considered before the interview. Reviewing the data over several weeks, I discovered three types of emotion work the teachers reported carrying out: emotion management; teachers' embodied work in classrooms; and explicit teaching of emotions. I discuss each of these in the Data Analysis section of this chapter with examples from the interview transcripts.

To frame the data analysis I next offer a selected review of the literature on teachers' emotions/affect in two parts: emotion work and bodies in classrooms. The section on emotion work includes a brief discussion of Hochschild's research, research on emotion work among writing program administrators and Zembylas's ethnography focused on an early-childhood science teachers' emotion work. The section on teachers' embodied work includes both feminist concepts of emotions as embodied and the work of affect theorists based on Deleuzian concepts, previously discussed in chapters 2 and 5, but taken up here in their relationship to the interplay between bodies in classrooms. The related literature is followed by the data analysis. The chapter ends with implications of the findings on teachers' emotion work for critical teaching, including suggestions about making room for "ugly feelings" (Ngai 2005).

Related Literature: Emotion Work

Hochschild's Research

> By "emotion work" I refer to the act of trying to change in degree or quality an emotion or feeling. To "work on" an emotion or feeling is, for our purposes, the same as "to manage" an emotion or to do "deep acting."
>
> (Hochschild, 1979, p. 561)

Much of the literature on teachers' emotions considered from a critical perspective pays tribute to Hochschild's pioneering work, especially her related terms: emotion work, emotional labor, emotion management, and feeling rules. Hochschild's contribution was to propose relationships among social factors and emotions, focusing on what people feel and on "what people think and do about what they feel" (Hochschild 1979, p. 552), including feeling rules driving those processes.

The concept of emotion management, work, or labor, has to do with people consciously trying to change the way they feel so that they might experience the "appropriate" emotion for a particular social context. An often-cited example of emotional labor from Hochschild's own research is her study of the training of airline attendants, 85 percent of which were female at the time, the late 1970s. Hochschild (1983) discovered that the job required not just physical and mental exertion, but also types of emotional labor emphasized repeatedly in the job training, including enacting a reassuring presence by smiling for the duration of a flight. Hochschild views this emotion management as the struggle between what the worker actually feels and what she is required to demonstrate outwardly, guided by feeling rules. She describes this as a process of calling up or suppressing particular emotions so as to maintain a prescribed outward appearance "that produces the proper state of mind in others – in the sense of being cared for in a convivial and safe place" (p. 7).

One of Hochschild's major points about emotional labor is that it is unrecognized and uncompensated, guided by a combination of explicit training and both tacit and explicit feeling rules.

Research on WPAs' Emotion Work

References to Hochschild's study are common in the literatures on emotions and education (Boler 1999; Hargreaves 2001; Jacobs and Micciche 2003; Micciche 2002, 2007; Zembylas 2005, 2007a, 2007b). One such literature analyzes the contradictions and complexities of the work of writing program administrators (WPAs), who oversee composition courses, train teachers and tutors, meet with students, tutor, teach, and so on. Beyond these more overt aspects of their work is the hidden emotional labor they carry out that goes unacknowledged and uncompensated, yet is often more taxing.

Micciche (2007), for example, reports on a survey she carried out on the affect and work of 22 WPAs. She uncovered a vast range of emotions resulting from simultaneously doing satisfying intellectual work and navigating the contradictions between institutions' explicitly stated goal of promoting academic literacy and underfunding writing programs. Micciche's respondents' emotion work therefore consisted of continually defending their programs to faculty across the curriculum and administrators, along with having to disappoint students and instructors they interacted with regularly by telling them, for example, that they couldn't enroll in certain courses, teach courses at particular times, or that their poor evaluations might lead to non-reappointment.

Nonetheless, rather than being overwhelmed and deflated by the challenges of their emotional labor, respondents reported that these challenges sometimes spurred them to act in their own, their colleagues', and their students' interests. That is, an aspect of emotion work was to deploy the tensions and contradictions as triggers for action. According to Micciche, then, emotion management among WPAs should not be seen simply as suppression of negative reactions to difficult situations or feeling rules, as Hochschild's more deterministic notion might suggest. Rather, Micciche's respondents seemed to consciously manage their emotions in the service of a healthy "emotional culture around writing," one that acknowledged obstacles and tensions while offering "leadership in support of innovative pedagogical practices" (p. 83). Emotion work, she claims, prevents alienation and highlights WPAs' struggles as inextricably personal and political. It should therefore be acknowledged and cultivated in healthy ways to prevent burnout and to enhance WPAs' administrative and pedagogical experiences.

Similarly, Holt, Anderson, and Rouzie (2003) examined daily emotion work carried out by WPAs in their institutions in lean times. The social context of emotional labor was multifaceted, including not just underfunding but these other aspects as well: contested definitions of literacy; how to employ new technology; justifying their work to colleagues who expected first-year composition courses to solve students' writing problems; translating composition scholarship to literary scholars, and so on. According to Holt et al, "[n]egotiating these boundaries" entailed "sophisticated emotion work, labor that is more often accomplished than acknowledged" (p. 151).

Focusing mainly on women in WPA positions, the authors note that unlike their male counterparts, females in these positions had to avoid expressing strong emotions, such as anger, even when they were opposed to policies they had to enforce. Their institutional role as nurturers, maternal figures who were to be a calming presence, conflicted with their view of themselves as activists intent on enacting curricular and institutional reforms. Therefore their emotion work included mediating tension between their "outlaw emotions" (p. 156) and the unspoken mandate that women maintain a pleasant and supportive demeanor at all times, much like the flight attendants in Hochschild's study.

Despite these findings, however, Holt et al. do not posit feeling rules in those contexts as deterministic. They find, instead, that female WPAs' emotion work is invisible, time-consuming and draining because they have shouldered the work quietly and therefore receive little, if any, assistance from colleagues. The authors hope that research such as theirs on emotion work might provoke a reckoning of its costs and benefits and eventually lead to it spreading across institutions so that it might be shared equally by men, women, faculty, administrators, staff, etc. This would shift the burdens and pleasures of emotion work from one sector to many with the promise of greater job satisfaction and personal relationships in the workplace for all.

Emotion Work of an Early Childhood Science Teacher

A comprehensive example of emotion work in the educational literature is Zembylas's (2005) ethnography of an early childhood science teacher, Catherine. Using a Foucauldian framework, he discusses her emotional labor as a negotiation of emotional rules, classroom relationships, mandated curricula, and her own notion of science as a collaborative and joyful process. Although at times in laying out his theoretical position Zembylas seems to subscribe to emotional rules as deterministic, at other times they seem negotiable and contingent. From a more deterministic perspective, Zembylas describes emotional rules in education as insidiously inexplicit: "disguised as ethical codes, professional techniques, and specialized pedagogical knowledge" (p. 52). In addition, he finds them, from a Foucauldian perspective, encoded in school architecture, the division of time into class period and "procedures of reward and punishment of teachers' pedagogies" (p. 56).

On the other hand, his analysis leaves open the possibility of resistance to emotional rules, offering Catherine as an example of teachers he considers "rule breakers" (p. 131). In fact, Zembylas suggests that "nonconformity to prevailing emotional rules demands emotional labor" (p. 57), an interesting finding about teachers' emotion work that mirrors an aspect of what the research on WPAs uncovered: conformity and nonconformity to emotion rules can be equally demanding of teachers' time and energy. Both are therefore important to attend to as aspects of teachers' emotion work.

Like those who studied the emotional labor of WPAs, Zembylas calls for further research on emotional rules and resistance in teaching so that the "oppressive and unequal effects" (p. 206) of these rules could be contested. Ideally, in his opinion, these discussions could lead to transformation of schools' emotional cultures to more democratic and open ones. He believes that if emotion work were considered more centrally, teachers could develop "emotional affinities" (p. 133) among themselves, leading to coalition building and reform.

Related Literature: Bodies in Classrooms

> I am seeking … to re/member pedagogical work as inescapably corporeal, involving fleshy bodies, with all the pluses and minuses that this can mean for classroom practice.
>
> (McWilliams, 1996, p. 367)

Those who take up teachers' and students' embodied emotions from a critical perspective focus both on the problems of bodies in the classroom and the importance of acknowledging their place and meaning. Bodies are problematic in part, according to this literature, because of the prohibition against sexual contact between teachers and students. Given the widespread agreement about the "wrongness of any sexual engagement between teachers and students," bodies in classrooms have been shut down (Probyn 2004, p. 37). This is particularly true for women academics who, Levy (2000) claims, are "defined by an empty bodily space (otherwise she becomes or is her body)" (p. 85). In other words, it is assumed that female academics will choose mind over body by adopting a safe motherly role to offset the forbidden one of seducer. A concern Levy raises about this choice is that as classroom nurturers, female professors are expected to give but not receive nurturing in return. Their unacknowledged desire for recognition and connection can thereby lead to diminishment of potential professional power.

For her part, McWilliams (2000) worries that the neoliberal "makeover of schools and colleges along corporate lines" (p. 27) excludes teachers as passionate and dramatic orators, an aspect of corporeal expression. Instead teachers are steered to act as skilled managers who develop learning products: online courses, syllabi, coursepacks, and so on. McWilliams traces this shift in teachers' roles to the work of humanist psychologists, such as Rogers and Maslow, who paved the way for a focus on learners/learning and away from teaching "as a personality cult … authoritarian or top down" (p. 32). The result has been that teachers are expected to be directors of learning whose bodies are erased due to a lack of interest in their performance per se. Instead, attention has shifted to students' performance, increasingly defined in neoliberal terms as predetermined learning outcomes, following the corporate model of accountability.

Given that learning outcomes are usually measured *after* learning has been facilitated, teachers' in-class actions and utterances are becoming irrelevant, according to McWilliams, especially when it comes to distance learning. Putting it even more dramatically, she believes that teachers' bodies are increasingly seen as "stumbling blocks" to be "stepped around, over, or on" (p. 32).

Backing up her claim that humanism and corporatism have been partnered to exclude teachers' bodies, McWilliams reports on a study she carried out with 100 postgraduate teachers to whom she posed the question, "What is education for and what are you for in education?" The vast majority reported that their task as educators was to raise students' self-esteem, a finding confirming McWilliams's belief that teachers in this neoliberal age have been trained to simultaneously pathologize and love their students, but in a narrow, sanitized way focused on repairing what is assumed to be their damaged self-regard. Left out of this equation is any unforeseen, messy outpouring of strong untamed emotions. In their place is the self-regulated role of teachers as "missionaries" whose job is to love thinly and wisely by "managing, missioning, mothering, and measuring students' bodies" (p. 36).

On the other hand, McWilliams (1996) does not call for a return to traditional authoritarian teaching, but, instead, a reckoning with teaching as a "lived and palpable experience of desire, pleasure, and pain" (p. 369). This construct is a challenge to the neoliberal one of teaching as a data delivery system and/or self-esteem raising process grounded in the assumption that students are mentally fragile and need teachers' psychological care. It also supplants the use of terms such as "motivation" that sanitize teaching and proposes, in their place, "desire" with its welcoming of "uncertain and transgressive ways" (p. 371) of bodies in classrooms. (p. 371). McWilliams's reference to "desire" entails greater attention to the "pedagogical body" (p. 374); that is, teachers and students not as overtly sexualized or eroticized, but, rather, as mutually self-interested in the process of becoming, with unpredictable outcomes.

Watkins (2006), too, is concerned about the erasure of teachers' bodies, given the focus on student-centered learning. Applying a Deleuzian framework to her study of writing instruction in an Australian middle school in a class of mostly English language learners, she found that the teacher she observed was quite directive in her encounters with students, giving explicit instruction about invention, textual forms, and techniques.

Watkins concludes from her research that there are three types of "pedagogic affect" which she defines as "the impact of bodies affecting bodies" (p. 272): discipline; praise; and contagion. As to discipline, that is, "force with an enabling potential" (p. 279), she refers to the positive results of the teacher's detailed instruction before and during lessons as well as her forceful presence in the classroom. Praise, and criticism, were also ever-present, leading to intense teacher/student interaction, but also affective contagion. Watkins concludes that the teacher's directive embodied style imposed on students in helpful ways, inciting them to write and improve their writing in ways that student-centered pedagogies might not have.

Also grounded in a Deleuzian approach and a critique of neoliberal educational policies is Probyn's (2004) discussion of bodies not as monolithic, but as assemblages of "an infinite number of particles, continually arranged and re-arranged in relations of speed and slowness" (p. 37). Conceptualizing bodies as broken up makes space for the unexpected, "the always quirky, always unknowable combination that is the classroom" (p. 37). Probyn calls for "micro-analysis of movement, gesture, and behavior" (p. 37) as a way to attend to how "bits of bodies connect (or don't)" (p. 37), offering the following examples of what bits might be noticed: eye contact; body movements; blushing; whispering; confessions; stuttering; facial tics. If attended to, these "small fragments" (p. 38) can reveal unexpected connections to course content and to other humans in the classroom.

While the literatures I reviewed on emotion work and bodies in classrooms differ, they share the common aim of taking teachers' emotional labor and bodies into account, especially female teachers'. Whether proposing greater attention to emotion work and emotional rules, more equitable sharing of emotion work, passion, desire, or bodies as assemblages, all call for more research on the role of teachers' and students' emotions and/or affect in classroom life.

Data Analysis

> You have to be all there. It can be physically and emotionally draining some days. You're thinking about each person in the class and how they're feeling. If someone is distracted, sleepy, bored, restless my first tendency is to think I'm not making the class interesting. But I do feel responsible to interest them ... I still think about what they're thinking about me: whether I'm completely prepared, with them. You're standing, pacing, gesturing, walking to the board. Everyone's looking at you and every once in a while they'll comment about what you're wearing. That reminds me all eyes are on me. You're responsible for their reactions, learning, interest. It's tied up with self-regard. If it's a great class, I'm high. If it's not so great I'm down: Am I a good teacher, person? Your identity is tied up with all this. I'm worrying about them. I'm worrying about myself: Am I a good teacher?

The quote above from one of my interviewees reveals that this English language teacher performs extensive emotion work in the classroom: trying to guess at students' states of mind and feelings; wondering whether the material is holding their interest; noticing students' bodily dispositions; wondering what the students think about her; noticing being watched; wondering about whether the class is going well and how that reflects on her as a teacher and human being. Emotional labor indeed.

The emotions most often chosen by the interviewees from the list of 22 were: happiness/joy; enthusiasm; compassion; caring; frustration; fascination; pride. Guilt and sadness/grief were each chosen once and empathy was added to the list by one interviewee. When analyzing the interview data I discovered three categories of emotion work: emotion management; teachers' embodied work; and explicit teaching of emotions. I discuss each of these separately next, including the sub-categories where relevant. I've chosen not to include information in this discussion about teachers' gender, race, age, or other aspects of their identities because this is not part of the analysis. I'm not trying to correlate identity and emotion work; rather I examine the data discursively, with the examples and analysis demonstrating the types of discourses that seemed to circulate around emotions and English language teaching among the teachers I interviewed.

Emotion Management

The two categories of emotion management revealed by the interview data are: 1) consciously working to bring emotions in line with what are considered "appropriate" emotions for teaching, or confirming that appropriate or useful emotions are in place; 2) managing emotions related to reading and/or writing assessment tests. I take up each next.

"Appropriate" Emotions

What characterizes this type of emotion work is a struggle between what teachers are feeling and what they believe they ought to be feeling while they're teaching. Feeling rules seem to be operating loosely, with no specific emotional destination or ideal state where teachers reported they were supposed to end up or convey to students. In addition, guiding their emotions in a different direction didn't necessarily mean the difficult emotion was replaced or erased. However, the self talk teachers reported carrying out about emotions in the classroom seemed to revolve around minimizing anger and impatience toward students. There was a sense that these teachers carry a deep awareness of the challenge their immigrant students face and they therefore strive to avoid making their lives even more difficult or stressful. In fact, anger, impatience, and blame seemed to be indicators to the teachers that they were pointed in the wrong direction, a signal for them to change course and go somewhere else:

> R1: When I'm angry I start to lecture, overexplain why I'm angry, that they should behave. I try to stand outside myself, "Shut up; drop it; this is unproductive" ... It bothers me. I feel like I have to explain better. I feel it's been damaging, that I may have to change directions, materials, set them in a different direction.

In R2, the teacher notices that the guilt she feels about not reading her students' papers is making her feel other unpleasant emotions, related to blaming her students for feeling guilty. So she stops herself from finding fault with them, yet her guilt does not disappear. In this case, the problem of trying to read student papers is related to growing class size; having an unreasonable number of students makes reading their papers increasingly difficult, leading the teacher to feel guilty and overworked:

> R2: When I feel guilty I feel irritated. Sometimes I take it out on them. I'm broody, bitchy, temperamental. I act as if *they* did something wrong. That makes me feel more guilty, guiltier, and guiltier. I can't do this again, not reading their papers, not giving them back what I was supposed to … I'm standing in the classroom berating myself. I'm not teaching them the way I want to be teaching. I'm too caught up, too consumed by guilt.

R3 describes an emotional trajectory surrounding classroom events not working out as expected. The teacher notices her frustration, tries to forgive her students for their "limitations" and then reminds herself that immigrant students often lack control over their situations: "[t]hey didn't choose to be here"; "teachers they had before"; "crappy placement"; and notions about language needing to be "correct." This is a clear example of a teacher's awareness of the social/emotional context of immigrant students' lives as a pedagogical guide, and attention to not adding to the challenges they face:

> R3: I'm alert to it [frustration]. I'm going out of control, feels unprofessional, like I'm being maternal in a bad way. Things you forgive your kid for, limitations … I check my source of frustration against the reality of the situation: what did I expect? They didn't choose to be here; they're not my children … Frustration is sensing the limits of what might happen, being aware of elements I have no control over: teachers they had before; crappy placement; language is about being correct.

On the other hand, another interesting aspect of management toward "appropriate" emotions was teachers monitoring their speech and comportment to avoid infantilizing English language learners by talking down to them or being too lax, as the next two responses indicate. What's notable about these is that they mention the concern that English language teachers can be *too* caring toward their students, knowing the obstacles they face as learners and diasporic people. In R4, the teacher works to balance her caring with reminders that her students are adults. She modulates her voice accordingly, being aware that speaking too clearly could be perceived as condescending. This is an interesting example both of teachers' emotion management and embodiment, discussed further in the next section of the data analysis:

> R4: ESL teachers seem to feel responsible for more: are they feeling comfortable, homesick, have trouble with the system? We're caring to

an extra length than in most disciplines. But we have to be careful not to treat them like children, talking down to them. I try to speak clearly, but then I worry that it will sound as if I'm talking down to them, as if they're children. It's a balance.

In R5, the teacher expresses pride in her reputation as a compassionate teacher. Yet she wonders whether her compassion is too great, interfering with "standards," something she struggles with as a mother:

> R5: I've gotten great feedback as a result of my compassion. I have a great rapport with students, a certain unspoken loyalty. I'll see them in the street: "You were my favorite." But I question it: Maybe I care too much. I'd like to be firmer. I let my compassion get in the way of my standards. I was a straight A student, but I didn't have compassionate teachers. I struggle with this as a mother. I let compassion get in the way of discipline.

Emotion management, then, seemed for these teachers to be a matter of sparing their students from anger, blame, and frustration while being mindful not to be infantilizing, lax, or condescending. Finding the right balance seemed to be a part of their emotion work.

Managing Emotions Related to Reading and/or Writing Assessment Tests

The responses in this category most clearly demonstrated the emotional impact of literacy testing on the teachers and their students. Teachers' sense of frustration comes through clearly in a few ways. One is the capricious nature of literacy tests that make it hard to predict who will pass and who will fail, conveyed in R9. Another is the way that teacher identity may be too closely tied to students' test results, poignantly discussed in R7 where the teacher questions her competency when her students fail. R6 and R8 revolve around teachers' obligation to comfort and reassure students when they fail.

This latter aspect of emotion management is important to attend to because though the tests are mandated, no provisions are made institutionally to deal with the emotional toll that failure takes on students and teachers. Instead, teachers take up the emotional slack, both their own and their students'. They encourage students by cheering them on while they're preparing for the tests, cheering them up when they fail, and urging them not to give up despite the difficulty of juggling work, family, and college with its literacy tests blocking access to credit-bearing courses. The additional toll on teachers of shouldering the burden of their own sense of failure when students don't pass assessment tests is yet another area of unacknowledged emotion work:

> R6: When students succeed you feel wonderful. When only four students passed the writing test ... I felt I hadn't fulfilled my goal. I take on the

> burden of their frustration. … I understand their pain and disappointment. I'm nervous when I get the scores. The only time I feel discouraged is when they fail the tests. It's really tough. I give them words of encouragement.
>
> R7: The failure rate is higher with ESL students no matter how much you do. There's a certain helplessness when scores come in. I start to question if I did my job. I one-hundred percent question myself. These reactions help me re-evaluate how I can be a better teacher next semester. They help me think about what I could have done to allow for more success.
>
> R8: I can tell when students are sad about their scores. They cry to me sometimes after class. I never know whether it's appropriate. I tell them, "It's ok. Sometimes it takes a few tries. You're lucky you're here in America. It's a great opportunity. Don't get discouraged." After class they express their grief, frustration. I say, "Keep trying."
>
> R9: Often a big cause of frustration is wondering why they failed in the first place. For example, in my current writing class there's a tremendous writer and I have no idea how she failed the first time. It's gonna be a pass this time, but how did she get put into this ESL track? When they give you stories of how hard they're working, taking care of younger siblings, keep getting 69 [one point below the passing score on the reading test], why can't they let me continue? … These are things we can't change.

The final comment in R9 offers food for thought. It speaks to the resignation teachers may experience about assessment tests, viewed as inevitable, "things we can't change." This is coupled with the way in which assessment instruments function as tests not just of students, but of teachers as well. "When students succeed, you feel wonderful," the teacher in R6 reports. On the other hand, if they fail, R7 expresses, "I start to question if I did my job." They may also question whether they will keep their job.

Emotion management related to testing, for some of the interviewees, centers on both resignation about the presence of literacy tests and their sense of responsibility about student performance. The problem with the resignation/responsibility formulation is that it leaves no room for opposition to testing and tracking. When teachers fulfill the unspoken mandate to rally students' enthusiasm about taking the tests and buoy their spirits when they fail, they might be contributing to the type of capitulation institutions count on to keep students' indignation and outrage about literacy tests in check.

This is not to suggest that teachers should stop mediating their students' emotions about tests; to do so would be inhumane. However, I believe that if students' concerns about literacy testing were examined more closely in class rather than assuaged and smoothed over privately, possibilities for reform of testing policies could be encouraged. I discuss this further in the implications section of the chapter.

Teachers' Embodied Work in Classrooms

Teachers' Embodied In-class Emotions

In this section I will explore three aspects of the data related to bodies in classrooms: McWilliams's notion of teaching as a "lived and palpable experience of desire, pleasure, and pain" (p. 369); Watkins's notion of embodiment as contagion; and Deleuze's notion of becoming, when teachers and students step out of their customary roles in unexpected ways. These data demonstrate the close connections between teachers' emotion work, their bodies, and their students' embodied emotions and affect.

As to teaching as a "lived and palpable experience of desire, pleasure, and pain," teachers discussed teaching as energizing, rejuvenating, joy feeding further joy, exemplified in the following responses:

> R10: Even if I feel tired, I feel a burst of energy that goes on after class. ... When I teach in the evening, I can go on till 11pm.
> R11: It gives me a sense, an adrenaline rush, like I'm performing.
> R12: They keep me coming back. It's rejuvenating to see how they respond to the English language.
> R13: When things are going well, there's joy and the joy feeds the teaching. When students ask questions that feeds the feeling and the feeling feeds the whole thing. It's circular.
> R14: You become part of them. You can touch them and feel what they're feeling and say, "Let's express this."

In addition, there were references to teachers and students influencing or catching each others' feelings, lending support for Watkins's claim that contagion is a feature of embodied emotions in classrooms. In fact, some teachers actually used the words "contagious" or "contagion" in their responses. This aspect of emotion work shows how carefully these teachers and their students seem to monitor each others' emotional states by reading each others' bodies:

> R15: It's important for me to be fascinated because it's contagious. For those whose English is limited or tend not to be interested in reading and writing, when they see my enthusiasm, some go back and read it. They hadn't known it was so interesting.
> R16: If I can't get to that place [compassion], I'm not there and the students notice and comment on it.
> R17: I try to be excited about anything I teach. If I'm not excited, they're not.
> R18: There are those moments when it's copacetic. I smile, laugh, try to mirror their enthusiasm, so it's infectious.

As to becoming, two teachers referenced moments in the classroom when there was a flow of teaching energy or students' excited reactions and to work with each other, described as "non-linear," "unchecked," "buzzing," and "magic moments." In fact, in R20, the teacher reflects on how during those moments she might feel "left out" as the teacher in her usual role, but then gauging the mood of the group, reminds herself that "this is good":

> R19: Part of ESL teaching is that in the classroom environment feeling can happen. It's non-linear, moments with humans, exchanges. I can relax and let the teaching come through me, unchecked moments.
>
> R20: There are magic moments when they all get excited, say smart things. I say to myself, "This is the way it's supposed to be." In groups or pairs they're doing it, buzzing, engaging with material … I try to get their attention, almost feel left out, but remind myself that, no, this is good.

One teacher described particularly touching moments in which students stepped out of their customary molar lines of the teacher/student binary, becoming protectors of the teacher and other students, guided by compassion:

> R21: They feel compassion for me sometimes. When I get frustrated, they realize they've pushed me over the edge by talking too much. They tap each other, shove each other and say, "Shut up. She's trying to tell us something." It isn't pity; it's compassion and they write about it. They say, "When x was giving her speech and her hands were shaking, I felt sorry for her and I wished I could stand next to her and do it for her."

Aside from students demonstrating friendship toward their teacher in R21, also interesting is how she reads their bodies ("They tap each other, shove each other.") and how they read each others' ("her hands were shaking"). More examples of this type of attention to bodies follow in the next section.

Teachers' Reading Emotions on Students' Bodies, Including Possible Misreadings

This was a type of emotion work that all my interviewees discussed. Granted, the interview question that elicited the following responses was: "How can you tell when students feel x?" However, I was surprised at the extent to which these teachers seemed to monitor the "small fragments" (Probyn 2004, p. 38) of their students' bodies for clues about how their classes were going. This embodied emotion work included attention to posture, eye contact, facial expressions, and tone of voice, as indicators of particular emotions, attention or inattention, comfort, and so on:

> R22: I can tell when students feel anxious because of their body language. They're more stiff; they don't talk to anybody. At the first meeting they don't know what to expect. Some are incoming freshmen so this

is their first interaction. Around the third week, you can see them loosen up. They talk to other students; they're more playful; their bodies are looser.

R23: When students feel guilty they look down. They won't make eye contact when I say, "Did everyone remember to read page x to page y?", they'll slap their foreheads. They act too cool for school, like they don't give a shit. They squirm and wiggle.

R24: They wait for each after class; they go home with each other. Males take females home because they worry about them at night. When they speak, they pause and look at each other, showing compassion, consideration.

R25: I can tell they're happy by the expression on their faces, their tone of voice. They're quick to respond, enthusiastic. They raise their hands, they say they're happy in their writing, that they feel good, making progress.

R26: You can tell when students are bored by the way they're sitting, checking cell phones, look on their faces, falling asleep.

R27: Ear to ear smiles.

R28: The way they offer help: sharing a book, lending a pen, leaning over and talking, catching someone up who comes in late (I wait a minute to see if someone will offer), asking someone to look up a word ... They share information, advice. I see it in their body language: turning toward each other, eye contact, sit close to share a book, turn chairs, climb over tables.

On the other hand, some teachers discussed being careful not to attribute too much meaning to students' bodies because of the possibility of misreading their emotions. Their concern about possible misreadings indicates a sophisticated and nuanced type of emotion work requiring noticing emotion on bodies, trying to read them, and simultaneously being mindful that emotions are difficult to ascertain:

R29: I can tell if students are happy for the most part. There's an energy though I don't know if it's happiness.

R30: When students heard my accent they looked at me with mistrust. They don't say it; I see it in their eyes. Maybe they don't. Maybe it's me.

R31: I know when they're angry about the reading, materials, other students. I keep an eye on them. They become short, withdrawn, make expressions. They might decide to leave the classroom, as if they have to go to the bathroom at that minute. There are little signs. But you can confuse anger with their not understanding. I try not to make assumptions. Sometimes I've said, "I can see this is making you angry," but it was a misreading. They hadn't understood.

R32: I used to think I could tell if students were happy. Now I'm not sure. ... Sometimes I feel I know, but then someone who seemed unhappy says I was the best professor they'd ever had. Students have gotten more complicated. I'm less confident that I know, but on the whole I know. By their demeanor, facial expressions, what they write about, whether they're attentive, interested. If they seem unhappy, I'm not sure whether it's the class or something personal. If they come late, it doesn't necessarily mean they're unhappy with the class.

Explicit Teaching of Emotions

The final theme I'll discuss that emerged from the data was that many of the teachers reported explicitly teaching particular emotions, including excitement, pride, compassion, and caring. This is not to say they offered lessons focused on those emotions; rather, emotion teaching was embedded in teaching other things or when incidents arose in the classroom, such as students showing a lack of compassion for each other. Emotion lessons were taken up along the way, but the teaching of emotions was explicit:

R33: If anything I teach them that learning is exciting: See, doesn't this feel good (the learning)? See, you're thinking really hard. You've had this ah-ha moment. I go meta.

R34: Pride is involved: Take the time to turn in work you think will pass, something you wrote on the bus is a waste of both our time. Don't throw it away, keep it in your piles, have pride in everything you do. I tell them I still have high school assignments.

R35: If they lack compassion I would probably get angry and talk to them about how to behave. You get what you give. That's a bedrock of community.

R36: Compassion is related to cross-cultural understanding. I'm trying to teach them if someone does something unexpected, it might be normal for them. If they find it offensive, they should try to imagine another interpretation. I have to do that a lot: "Don't tell him to shut up! He's trying to say it in a way that's normal in his culture"; "Don't tell her she has to stand."

R37: I teach them caring, but I don't call it caring. It's about how we respond to others, the gift of education, what they should do to help others. Corny things: do you tell your parents you appreciate that they're giving you an education?

These responses, and all the earlier ones about teachers' emotion work, point to a need in ELT to consider teachers' emotion work in classrooms, part of the fabric of their interactions, judgments, teaching, and learning. If it's true, as my data suggest, that teachers are managing their emotions by struggling to find the right ones for teaching, they need support in that struggle. If it's true that teachers are expected to handle the emotional fallout from students failing assessment tests, this emotion work also needs to be acknowledged if not assigned to other personnel, such as counselors or testing officials.

The embodied emotional labor that teachers carry out also needs great attention, including desire, pleasure, and pain. Their scrutiny of students' bodies as indicators of interest, engagement, boredom, fascination, and so on also needs to be addressed. How explicit teaching of emotions intersects with teaching language is another area requiring further research.

Implications for Critical English Language Teaching

Critical ELT and Ugly Feelings

> We are interested in the potential for "bad feelings" like hopelessness, apathy, anxiety, fear, numbness, despair, and ambivalence to constitute and be constituted as forms of resistance. While we are all too aware of how the state and the media mobilize and manipulate emotions to produce a loyal citizenry and prosecute the "war on terrorism," we are also critical of the ways in which the left and social movements relegate emotions to the so-called "private" or "individual" sphere. In opposing the facile splitting of thinking and feeling, we are for a pedagogy of complex feelings, for a surrealist and imaginative politics that embraces ambivalence, the ridiculous, and the raw.
>
> (www.feeltankchicago.net)

> Depressed? ... It Might Be Political.
>
> (Berlant, 2004b, p. 451)

One thing that struck me about the interviews with teachers was how most of the emotions discussed were not of the "bad" type described in the quote from feeltankchicago.net. This may have been because after asking teachers to select the emotions they experienced most commonly in the classroom, I asked them to narrow their choice to three. Had I interviewed them about all the originally selected emotions, I might have learned more about the "bad feelings."

Nevertheless, there did seem to be an overall sense that part of teachers' emotion work was to be cheerful and to cheer students up. In fact, one interviewee asked me jokingly why there wasn't an emotion on the list related to being a cheerleader. So, I'll start this final section of the chapter on teachers' emotion work with an exploration of the idea that critical teaching might be enhanced if teachers encouraged greater attention to bad or ugly feelings rather than trying to suppress them in themselves and coax students out of them.

For this exploration, I return to Ahmed's notion of the happy migrant, discussed in Chapter 3. A quick reminder of that discussion: Ahmed raises questions about the requirement for those who migrate to immigrant-receiving countries to be happy. She attributes the happy migrant phenomenon to an unspoken mandate that immigrants continually demonstrate their gratitude for being permitted to settle in the new land. Immigrants with sour dispositions appear ungrateful instead of delighted by their reception, no matter how unwelcoming. Their unhappiness can also be read as a refusal to sever connections to the world they came from, along with speaking other languages, wearing identifiably "foreign" clothes, and interacting with compatriots. They are viewed as being pointed in the wrong direction when exhibiting unhappiness.

Though English language teachers are probably more thoughtful than most when it comes to cross-culture sensitivity, it's interesting to consider how we might get caught up in the happy migrant phenomenon, acting as cheerleaders of migration happiness. We may feel compelled to urge unhappy students to drop their bad feelings and adopt sunnier ones, as a way to show their appreciation for the ESL class, the teacher, or, more globally, "the opportunity." Two responses, in particular, struck me as demonstrating this type of emotion labor:

> R9: I can tell when students are sad about their scores. They cry to me sometimes after class. I never know whether it's appropriate. I tell them, "It's ok. Sometimes it takes a few tries. You're lucky you're here in America. It's a great opportunity. Don't get discouraged." After class they express their grief, frustration. I say, "Keep trying."
>
> R38: They come in very glum I ask, "Where's that smile?" It seems like their problems are all gone. I'm drawing them in.

Though I'm sympathetic to the desire to create a congenial classroom atmosphere, I'd like to argue for greater hospitality toward teachers' and students' ugly feelings, or a pedagogy of complex feelings, mentioned in the quote that opens this section. But before doing that, I'd like to acknowledge the possibility that maintaining a cheery disposition and cajoling students into cheeriness may, in part, be a result of neoliberal cutbacks. When looking over the data, I wondered whether the teachers I interviewed, particularly contingent ones, worried that students' unhappiness could threaten their employment, especially if students reported their unhappiness to supervisors. Is it possible that an aspect of teachers' emotional labor is to make students happy in order to avoid being fired? This is a question I include in the concluding chapter along with other implications for further research.

Returning to a pedagogy of complex feelings, I'd like to argue that forced cheeriness, though perhaps understandable for the reasons I just mentioned, risks thwarting opportunities for critical teaching. An alternative to coaxing students' smiles or asking them to exhibit gratitude for being in our class, or the immigrant-receiving country, would be to allow them to articulate their ugly feelings as a way to better understand their situations, including the challenges they face as immigrants and students whose education has been stalled by their exclusion from the mainstream. We can engage ELLs in a process that acknowledges their unhappy feelings as legitimate, rather than ones that need to be repressed or transcended. This process invites them to explore their feelings not as personal but political.

For example, I now begin each semester by asking students to write about their feelings concerning the assessment test that placed them in my ESL course. There are no happy feelings. Students are upset, confused, angry, embarrassed, overwhelmed, and sometimes despairing. After they share these feelings with the class, I tell them that their reactions are legitimate and common, as can be seen from their classmates' responses. I explain that the tests can be looked at in two ways, linguistically and politically. The linguistic explanation is that the tests are language-proficiency instruments that place them in English language courses so they can improve their reading and writing. The political explanation is that funding for public higher education, and the entire public sector, is diminishing and that the tests function to depress their aspirations so that they will lose hope and abandon their plans to get a college degree.

I also put the tests in a historical context by explaining that immigrants have traditionally been expected to do jobs that citizens don't want to do and that this expectation persists, though in a complicated way in a depressed economy, as seen by anti-immigrant backlash. If their aspirations are depressed by the tests and they give up, they will end up taking those jobs. I ask them what kinds of jobs they would have if they didn't go to college. They offer: driving taxicabs; working in retail; waiting tables in a restaurant; doing nails; taking care of other peoples' children. In fact, these are their jobs while attending college. I ask them what types of jobs they'd like to do after graduating and they tell me they want to open small businesses, be accountants, become teachers. I tell them not to be defeated by the tests, but that they're going to have to work very hard not to get swept up in their wake.

The exercise I just described could be viewed as a type of cheerleading because I'm urging my students not to allow the tests to stand in their way. But I never ask students to cheer up. I acknowledge their justified feelings, born from failing the assessment tests, and explain the neoliberal context that has reduced funding for public institutions and programs. I also assign readings about testing that offer varying perspectives about their uses and abuses. But rather than telling students not to be discouraged about the tests, I try to make space for unhappy migrants to express their unhappiness, giving "support to those who are unseated by the tables of happiness" (Ahmed 2010, p. 20).

In addition, by acknowledging students' feelings and exploring ways that they are legitimate and politically grounded, I hope I'm paving the way for them to become politically engaged as a result of understanding that the source of their unhappiness is something that is negotiable. I want my students to understand the politics of public higher education so that they will defend it for themselves and future generations. Asking them to abandon their ugly feelings and act like happy migrants would short circuit that possibility.

Conclusion

The data presented in this chapter point to an important yet overlooked area of English language teaching: teachers' emotion work and the role of their bodies, and students' bodies, in classrooms. Three themes emerged from my data. The first, emotion management, was further broken down into two sub-themes: 1) consciously working to bring emotions in line with what are considered "appropriate" emotions for teaching, or confirming that "appropriate" emotions are in place; and 2) managing emotions related to reading and/or writing assessment tests. The second theme, teachers' embodied work, was divided into two sub-themes: 1) teachers' embodied emotions; and 2) teachers' reading and possibly misreading students' bodies. The third theme was explicit teaching of emotions.

Given how readily and extensively teachers spoke about their emotions during the interviews, emotion work seems to be a vital area of further research. In addition, I hope this chapter will encourage greater attention in English language teaching programs to the emotion work carried out by teachers on a daily basis. Acknowledging this work would not only highlight its role in teaching, but could potentially cultivate what Micciche (2007) calls a healthy "emotional culture" (p. 83), one promoting open discussion of emotion work and recognizing both its challenges and rewards. In addition, an open emotional culture might produce what Zembylas (2005) calls "emotional affinities" (p. 133) between teachers, encouraging them to voice and welcome not just pretty feelings but also ugly ones, paving the way for institutional and pedagogical reforms.

8

WHAT REMAINS

Implications for Critical Teaching and Research

Story of J.

J. was routinely late for class, despite my repeated warnings that she risked exceeding the number of allowed latenesses. I also explained that her lateness was disruptive to me and her fellow students. In response she would say that she had chemistry lab before my class and sometimes had to stay after class to finish her work. I couldn't understand why this continued to be an issue, why she couldn't break away from the lab knowing that she had my class right after.

It was only at midterm, when students were doing an in-class assignment in which they evaluated the class that I discovered the fuller story. The assignment was to write answers to the following questions: What do you like most about the class? What do you like least? What suggestions do you have to improve the class? In response to the third question, J. offered three suggestions: "1) too strict on attendance. Just give more chances; 2) more reading practices; 3) actually I may know how to summarize, just give use suggestions how to catch the idea in short time?"

When students shared their responses, J. explained her reference to strict attendance in answering the third question, saying that she was late to class because her lab partner needed help with chemistry problems and that sometimes she didn't bring her lunch so J. offered hers. Then J. would come to class both late and hungry.

I open the concluding chapter with this anecdote because, like so many other incidents in my classes, this one encapsulates the emotional content of English language teaching and learning. The story of J. illustrates both my emotion work and my student's, including the complexity of J.'s emotions when navigating institutional requirements and barriers, demanding course work outside of ESL classes, and her sense of obligation to a peer. This anecdote illustrates teachers' and students' emotional calculations, trying to figure out the best use of their time and energy, given varying demands.

From my perspective, J.'s lateness was initially irritating. I found it intrusive and disrespectful, particularly given the fact that I continually reminded her that four latenesses equaled one absence and that she was permitted only seven hours of absence from my class, according to state regulations. In this situation I was both the enforcer of this policy and the hurt and concerned teacher who wondered why this capable and seemingly responsible student did not show more interest in my class or more maturity about attendance.

However, my feelings about the situation changed when I learned that the actual reason for J.'s chronic lateness was her desire to help a fellow student who was having difficulty with chemistry lab. It seemed that from J.'s perspective, helping this student was more urgent than going to my class, particularly because she wasn't even getting what she felt she needed to pass the reading test: more practice tests and suggestions for how to capture main ideas quickly.

An additional twist to this story was that the student who J. was helping needed assistance not only with chemistry but also with nutrition. So J. had taken on the role of both tutor and, perhaps, surrogate mother or big sister, sacrificing her own need for food in service of her tutee's.

Given J.'s explanation for her lateness, offered during the class discussion of their midterm evaluations, I could no longer view her tardiness as careless flouting of rules or indifference, but, instead, as an interesting conundrum. J. wanted to pass the reading test, as do all students who enroll in my ESL reading class. She was hoping to spend the semester in my class practicing for the reading test and learning how to identify main ideas quickly. Instead the ongoing assignment was to write response papers about a variety of articles that included a short summary, two questions about the article's content, a quote from the article and a written response to that quote, and definitions of unfamiliar words. Since J. felt that she already knew how to summarize articles, these response papers may have seemed like a waste of time rather than useful preparation for passing the reading test, her sole aim in taking the class even if I had larger goals in mind.

Once I had the bigger picture of J.'s lateness, my feelings of hurt and irritation began to shift to compassion and admiration along with shame that I wasn't giving her what she felt she needed, tempered by bewilderment that she didn't perceive the connection between writing summaries and understanding main ideas. Yet, at the same time, I got a glimpse of one of the numerous time pressures J. experienced: the need to "catch the idea in short time." Though the reading test is untimed, students have to read several passages and answer multiple-choice questions. It may therefore have been, from her perspective, that writing summaries, in which she felt sufficiently proficient, did not adequately mirror the skills required to quickly get main ideas from reading passages. Plus I had to remind myself that I'd asked for feedback about the class and, in a way, J.'s suggestion to figure out a way to teach students to get the main idea quickly was a gift, as long as I could set aside feeling embarrassed that I hadn't done this previously. On the other hand, adding to these feelings was my ongoing disgust at the multiple-choice reading test that degrades reading by reducing it to a handful of quantified skills, leading students to make requests for quick fixes, as J. had.

In addition, I had to consider the number of absences J. had accrued and make sure she did not exceed the maximum number and disqualify herself from retaking the reading test at the end of the semester, in accordance with university policy. That is, I was involved in my own complicated emotional calculus, juggling my compassion for and admiration of J., my concern about her attendance record, my embarrassment about having neglected to teach strategies for quickly accessing main ideas, my appreciation to J. for offering this suggestion, and my resentment, both toward the anti-intellectual climate created by the reading test and about having to enforce an attendance policy made by bureaucrats with no contact with the people they legislated about.

Fortunately J. and I were able to reach agreement by acknowledging the emotions we both had surrounding the attendance policy and our varying roles. I explained to her privately that I was impressed by her desire to help a fellow student and touched that she gave away her lunch. Yet, I told her that she had a responsibility to herself and to me that was greater than the one she exhibited to her lab partner. I also reiterated that she risked accruing so many absences that she would no longer qualify to retake the reading test. In addition, I thanked her for the suggestion to add techniques for locating main ideas quickly and told her I planned to incorporate some.

J. seemed moved by my acknowledgment of her actions, thoughtfulness, and suggestion and promised not to be late thereafter. She would eat her own lunch and ask her lab partner to bring her own. And that's what happened from then on.

Just as I began this book with a personal narrative, my social/emotional history, so I wrap it up with a story, this one from my teaching. In both I describe how I felt my way in dealing with events, gauging the emotional temperature of the situation and modifying my thoughts and emotions as I gained greater awareness. The type of emotion work I carried out with J. is common, judging from my informal chats and interviews with teachers. It should therefore be attended to in critical teaching and research in ways that honor the complexity of handling institutional requirements, social expectations, intellectual engagement, and classroom connections.

In the remainder of this concluding chapter I discuss the assumptions about emotions that I adopted in the book, the findings from the four Praxis chapters, and implications for critical teaching and research.

Assumptions about Emotions/Affect

There was a steep learning curve as I read about how emotions and affect have been theorized in various fields: sociology, anthropology, women's studies, geography, and so on. At times these works were dishearteningly obtuse, coded, and, to my mind, unnecessarily abstract. I longed for examples of the concepts the authors referenced, yet these were often absent. One important exception is the work of Sara Ahmed which I've discussed throughout the book because of its influence on my thinking about emotions as social constructs. Despite the intellectual challenges of absorbing the various literatures, I derived the following assumptions about emotion and affect, and their relationship to critical English language teaching and learning, the ones that drove my research and writing:

1. Emotions have mainly been ignored in scholarship, in part because they have been seen as subjective, irrational, exclusively female, and hard to capture; in ELT they have been constructed, for the most part, as exclusively cognitive;
2. Emotions are not private, individual, psychological states, but social and embodied. Emotions connect mind and body, acknowledging language teaching and learning as not only cognitive, not only social, but also physical;
3. Emotions are not static or monolithic, but, instead overlap, move, and shift. Therefore sorting them into negative and positive categories, as if some are good for language learning and others are bad, is a reductive way of considering them in English language teaching;
4. Intuitively and anecdotally emotions seem to factor into teaching and learning so it would be useful to understand them better.

Findings

Figuring out how to apply these assumptions and their attendant theories to practice was another challenge, reflected in the Praxis section of the book, each chapter of which offers a different perspective on emotions and/or affect and with a different population. The findings from the surveys and interviews I carried out, though tentative and open to further reflection and research, are:

1. Emotions stick to certain objects, including those used in English language teaching and learning, and are therefore worth exploring in classroom contexts for greater understanding of their role. When teachers and students have differing reactions to these objects, pulling them toward themselves or pushing them away, those differences can be important areas of exploration, leading to greater understanding of teaching and learning;
2. Teaching and learning are not only intellectual activities but also embodied ones. Provoking and/or attending to embodied responses can enhance teaching and learning, at times creating possibilities for transcending conventional teacher/student roles, sometimes encouraging lines of flight;

3. Inviting English language learners to come up with metaphors for English language learning can draw attention to ways that it is embodied and performative, possibly deepening students' engagement. Language acquisition students can also be asked to write metaphors based on their experiences learning additional languages, as a way to interrogate existing theories;
4. Emotions and affect are tools for understanding moment-by-moment pedagogical decision-making, grounded in teachers' and students' embodied reactions to classroom events;
5. Teachers carry out complex emotion work, entailing: managing their emotions to get to the "appropriate" ones; trying to read students' emotions on their bodies; explicitly teaching emotions;
6. Attention to emotions and affect theorizes critical teaching not for implausibly grand liberation, empowerment, or transformation, but, rather, as small and subtle shifts in perception or understanding that cumulatively might lead to social reform.

Remaining Questions

This book, like many, is incomplete. I could have gone on writing more about each chapter and even adding chapters. The relationship between emotions and critical English language teaching is a rich subject with many intriguing areas to explore. It is one I intend to continue studying by pursuing the following questions about critical English language teaching and research:

1. Which emotions, teachers' and students', stick to other objects that enter into play in ELT: quizzes, textbooks, writing assignments, grades, and so on? How can stickiness be explored so that these objects and the emotions sticking to them might be negotiated toward greater understanding and more productive engagement?
2. What is the role of film and other visual media in a pedagogy of affect? If, according to Kramsch, greater attention to other symbolic systems, such as electronic and cinematic ones, are tools that may help students explore multilingualism and embodiment, how can these resources be best used to cultivate those explorations?
3. How might contradictory aspects of individual emotions, such as compassion and withholding, be explored toward greater understanding of classroom events?
4. What are some ways to invite visceral reactions to texts, along the lines of Probyn's (2004) "goosebump effect," (p. 29) to engage a pedagogy of embodied emotions?
5. What drives teachers' obligation to manage their emotions in the classroom so that they constantly exude enthusiasm and caring? Does the cognitive mandate to strive for emotional literacy, emphasizing so-called

positive emotions, come into play? To what extent does neoliberalism, with its budget cuts and job insecurity influence emotion management, driving teachers, particularly contingent ones, to maintain a cheerful demeanor and cheer their students up? That is, with teachers increasingly seen as interchangeable product deliverers and the growing tendency of students, considered customers in the neoliberal paradigm, to register complaints about instructors, do teachers feel pressure to placate students in order to prevent job loss?

6. To what extent do English language teachers pathologize immigrant students, believing they have low self-esteem that needs to be boosted, a concern raised by McWilliams (2000)? How much do English language teachers feel obliged to give immigrant students the "gift of happiness" as part of a happiness mission (Ahmed 2010, p.125)? What types of relationships do these constructions forestall?

7. How can teachers acknowledge their own and students' "ugly feelings" (Ngai 2005) as an entrée to discussing the challenges of navigating the complexity of living in a globalized world in a time of neoliberal uncertainty?

8. What are ways to cultivate "emotional affinities" (Zembylas 2005, p. 133) between teachers in the same program, community, and the wider field as a way to jumpstart reforms that might improve teaching and learning conditions, particularly during this time of neoliberal austerity and cut backs? How might this type of collaboration that acknowledges emotion work as shared, not private, be a catalyst for organizing toward more favorable teaching and learning conditions?

9. What is the relationship between time and emotions? When students feel the pressures of juggling various work, family, and school demands, what is the role of emotions in these time constraints? How do we engage students in exploring that relationship?

10. How can English language teachers cultivate a larger repertoire of emotional discourses? For example, going back to the story of J., when I got stuck in the role of enforcer of the attendance policy, I adopted a discourse of hurt and indignation wondering how my student could flout the rules and blow off the beginning of my class. How might a wider range of discourses of emotions allow teachers to point themselves in the direction of students rather than toward institutional rules? How might this larger repetoire address invisible aspects of students' complicated lives that might affect their ability to engage in the ELT classroom? How might teachers investigate what else might be going on in students' lives from the perspective of other emotional discourses: curiosity, love, political awareness?

11. What can be done institutionally so that the entire burden of mediating students' emotional stress when failing assessment tests does not fall on their teachers who in turn must deal with their own emotional responses to their students not passing?

12. How can bodies in classrooms be acknowledged so that teachers become more aware of attending to their embodied emotions and reading emotions on their students' bodies? How might attention to bodies as assemblages be explored with students to cultivate awareness of language learning as embodied?

Finally ...

Working on this book was immensely satisfying because it incorporates areas I care about deeply: emotions, teaching, learning, language, politics, and dissent. Though it's taken me a while to unite these interests, I'm gratified to have had the opportunity to consider their interconnections.

As I've shown in this conclusion, each chapter of *Considering Emotions in Critical English Language Teaching: Theories and Praxis* suggests areas of further research and opportunities for praxis. I look forward to continuing this work myself, including discovering connections between theories and praxis that were invisible to me while writing this book. I hope that readers will draw my attention to those missed connections. Above all, I hope that the theories I describe and examples of their application to teaching will encourage others to consider emotions in their praxis, provoking the affective turn in critical English language teaching.

NOTES

Chapter 1

1 I use the terms emotions and affect interchangeably in this book, a choice I explain in Chapter 3 where I discuss the work of those who have made the same choice and those who distinguish them.
2 Robert Kennedy was assassinated on June 5, 1968 after midnight in California so I was not in school when this murder took place.
3 On the other hand, in Chapter 7, I discuss feminists' challenge to downplaying the role of teachers, and their bodies, an interesting critique of the convergence of humanism and neoliberalism.
4 To this day, when teaching language acquisition I do a shock language Silent Way French lesson with my students, using the sound/color and word charts and Cuisenaire rods. Those who have studied French observe the students participating in the lesson. The ensuing discussion is a chance for the observers and students to share their perceptions of what took place, adding to their understanding of language learning processes.
5 In Benesch (1993) I discuss a 1988 lawsuit filed by the Mexican American Legal Defense and Education Fund in California, Valdez vs. Randall, charging that literacy testing violated due process and equal protection guarantees for Hispanic students by excluding them from credit-bearing courses. According to Moore and Schulock (2007), the lawsuit led to the following changes: use of multiple measures for placement rather than a single score on a high-stakes test; establishing pre-requisites for particular courses on a case-by-case basis rather than across the curriculum; use of a basic skills course as a pre-requisite only if it has been established through "sound research practices" that a student is "highly unlikely to succeed in the course" (p. 27).
6 Vandrick (2009) acknowledges the tricky waters those with various types of privilege navigate when advocating for others. Yet, she urges not abandoning these battles out of fear of being perceiving as condescending. Instead, she offers important distinctions between speaking *for*, on the one hand, and speaking *with*, *about*, and *out for*, on the other.

Chapter 2

1 This is not an exhaustive review of applied linguistics publications that acknowledge emotions in language acquisition and/or use. So, I want to acknowledge two that offer

interesting insights, but are not included in the body of this chapter. The first is Prior's (2011) discursive analysis of anger expressed in his interviews of an adult immigrant narrating his difficult experiences with Canadian bank personnel. The other is Granger's (2004) psychoanalytic exploration of silence in second language acquisition.
2 Chun's (2009) critique of Goleman's emotional intelligence and its neoliberal assumptions is an important contribution to the critical EAP literature and a corrective to the mandate to encourage students to change their emotions so that they might be more "appropriate" even when their grievances are legitimate responses to unfavorable social conditions.

Chapter 3

1 The relationship between affect and emotion has been theorized in various ways. Some writers whose work I examined in the last chapter and will examine in this one make a clear distinction between the two, while others use the terms interchangeably. I keep them separate when exploring Deleuzian approaches to pedagogy, as in Chapter 5. At other times I use them interchangeably, a choice I touch on in Chapter 1 and explain more fully in this chapter.
2 Zemblyas asked Catherine to keep a diary in which she recorded emotions and moods, the first more fleeting and the second more lasting. He asked her to document whether what she experienced was an emotion or mood; to identify the type, for example, happiness/joy, anger/irritation, etc., and to discuss what was happening when it arose. In addition, the emotion diary was a place to record any bodily sensations and thoughts associated with the emotion or mood.

Chapter 4

1 This analysis of the calibration of hospitality is reminiscent of Berlant's (2004a) discussion of the relationship between compassion and withholding, discussed in Chapter 3.

Chapter 5

1 An earlier version of this chapter appeared in Nigel Harwood (ed.) (2010) *English Language Teaching Materials: Theory and Practice*. New York: Cambridge University Press.

REFERENCES

Ahmed, S. (2004a). *The cultural politics of emotion*. New York: Routledge.
Ahmed, S. (2004b). Affective economies. *Social Text, 79*, 117–39.
Ahmed, S. (2010). *The promise of happiness*. Durham NC: Duke University Press.
Albrecht-Crane, C. (2005). Pedagogy as friendship: Identity and affect in the conservative classroom. *Cultural Studies, 19*, 491–514.
Albrecht-Crane, C. and Stack, J. D. (2003). Toward a pedagogy of affect. In Stack, J. D. (ed.). *Animations of Deleuze and Guattari* (pp. 191–216). New York: Peter Lang.
Arnold, J. (ed.) (1999). *Affect in language learning*. New York: Cambridge University Press.
Arnold, J. and Brown, H. D. (1999). A map of the terrain. In J. Arnold (ed.). *Affect in language learning* (pp. 1–27). New York: Cambridge University Press.
Benesch, S. (ed.) (1988). *Ending remediation: Linking ESL and content in higher education*. Washington, DC: TESOL.
——(1992). Sharing responsibilities: An alternative to the adjunct model. *College ESL 2*, 1–10.
——(1993). ESL, ideology, and the politics of pragmatism. *TESOL Quarterly 27*, 705–17.
——(1999). Rights analysis: Studying power relations in an academic setting. *English for specific purposes 18*, 313–27.
——(2001). *Critical English for academic purposes: Theory, politics, and practice*. Mahwah NJ: Lawrence Erlbaum.
——(2006). Critical media awareness: Teaching resistance to interpellation. In J. Edge (ed.). *(Re)Locating TESOL in an age of empire* (pp. 49–64). Basingstoke, Hampshire: Palgrave Macmillan.
——(2007a). What about the students? English language learners in postsecondary settings. In J. Cummins and C. Davison (eds). *International handbook of English language teaching, Part II* (pp. 655–66). New York: Springer.
——(2007b). Critical praxis as materials development: Countering military recruitment on a U.S. campus. International Society for Language Studies Conference (ISLS), Honolulu.
——(2008). "Generation 1.5" and its discourses of partiality: A critical analysis. *Journal of Language, Identity, and Education 7*, 294–311.
——(2009). Interrogating in-between-ness: A postmodern perspective on immigrant students. In M. Roberge, M. Siegal, and L. Harklau (eds). *Generation 1.5 in college composition: Teaching academic writing to US-educated learners of ESL* (pp. 65–72). New York: Routledge.

—— (2010). Critical praxis as materials development: Responding to military recruitment on a US campus. In Nigel Harwood (ed.). *English language teaching materials: Theory and practice* (pp. 109–28). New York: Cambridge University Press.
Berlant, L. (2004a). Compassion (and withholding). In L. Berlant (ed.). *Compassion: The culture and politics of an emotion* (pp. 1–13). New York: Routledge.
—— (2004b). Critical inquiry, affirmative culture. *Critical Inquiry* 30, 445–51.
Boler, M. (1999). *Feeling power: Emotions and education*. New York: Routledge.
Braidotti, R. (2005). Affirming the affirmative: On nomadic affectivity, rhizomes 11/12, fall 2005/spring 2006. Retrieved from www.rhizomes.net/issue11/braidotti.html
Brown, C. (1965). *Manchild in the promised land*. New York: Touchstone.
Chun, C. W. (2009). Contesting neoliberal discourses in EAP: Critical praxis in an IEP classroom. *Journal of English for Academic Purposes* 8, 111–20.
Clarke, M. A. (1982). On bandwagons, tyranny, and common sense. *TESOL Quarterly* 16, 437–48.
Clough, P. T. (2007). Introduction. In P. T. Clough and J. Halley (eds). *The affective turn: Theorizing the social* (pp. 1–33). Durham NC: Duke University Press.
Colebrook, C. (2002). *Gilles Deleuze*. London: Routledge.
Combination Platter (2005), dir. Tony Chan. Port Washington NY: Koch Lorber Films.
Das kurze Leben des Jose Antonio Guitierrez (2006), dir. Heidi Specogna. New York: The Cinema Guild.
Davies, B., Pratt, C. C., Ellwood, C., Gannon, S., Zabrodska, K., and Bansel, P. (2009). Second skin: The architecture of pedagogical encounters. In B. Davies, B. and Gannon, S. (eds). *Pedagogical encounters* (pp. 131–49). New York: Peter Lang.
Deleuze, G. and Guattari, F. (1987). *A thousand plateaus: Capitalism and schizophrenia*. Minneapolis: University of Minnesota Press.
Dornyei, Z. and Malderez, A. (1999). The role of group dynamics in foreign language teaching and learning. In J. Arnold (ed.). *Affect in language learning* (pp. 155–70). New York: Cambridge University Press.
Ehrmann, M. (1999). Ego boundaries and tolerance of ambiguity in second language learning. In J. Arnold (ed.). *Affect in language learning* (pp. 68–86). New York: Cambridge University Press.
Freeman, D. and Johnson, K. (1998). Reconceptualizing the knowledge base of language teacher education. *TESOL Quarterly 32*, pp. 397–417.
Freire, P. (1970). *Pedagogy of the oppressed*. New York: Continuum.
Gattegno, C. (1963). *Teaching foreign languages in schools the Silent Way*. New York: Educational Solutions.
Goldstein, T. (2008). The capital of "attentive silence" and its impact on English language and literacy education. In J. Albright and A. Luke (eds). *Pierre Bourdieu and literacy education* (pp. 209–32). New York: Routledge.
Goleman, D. (2005). *Emotional intelligence*. New York: Bantam Books.
Golombek, P. R. and Johnson, K. E. (2004). Narrative inquiry as a meditational space: Examining emotional and cognitive dissonance in second-language teachers' development. *Teachers and Teaching: Theory and Practice 10*, 307–27.
Gorton, K. (2007). Theorizing emotion and affect: Feminist engagements. *Feminist Theory* 8, 333–48.
Granger, C. A. (2004). *Silence in second language learning: A psychoanalytic reading*. Clevendon: Multilingual Matters.
Grey, M. (2009). Ethnographers of difference in a critical EAP community-becoming. *Journal of English for Academic Purposes*, 8, 121–33.
Griffin, J. H. (1961). *Black like me*. New York: Houghton Mifflin.
Hardt, M. (2007). Foreword: What affects are for. In P.T Clough and J. Halley (eds). *The affective turn: Theorizing the social* (pp. viiii–xiii). Durham NC: Duke University Press.

Hargreaves, A. (2001). Emotional geographies of teaching. *Teachers College Record 103*, 1056–80.
Harris, O. (2010). Emotional and mnemonic geographies at Hambledon Hill: Texturing neolithic places with bodies and bones. *Cambridge Archaeological Journal 20*, 357–71.
Harwood, N. (ed.) (2010). *English language teaching materials: Theory and practice*. New York: Cambridge University Press.
Hemmings, C. (2005). Invoking affect: Cultural theory and the ontological turn. *Cultural Studies 19*, 548–67.
Hochschild, A. R. (1979). Emotion work, feeling rules, and social structures. *Journal of Sociology 85*, 551–75.
——(1983). *The managed heart: Commercialization of human feeling*. Berkeley: University of California Press.
——(2003). *The commercialization of intimate life: Notes from home and work*. Berkeley: University of California Press.
Hoffman, E. (1989). *Lost in translation: A life in a new language*. New York: E. P. Dutton.
Holborow, M. (2006). Ideology and language: Interconnections between neo-liberalism and English. In J. Edge (ed.). *(Re)Locating TESOL in an age of empire* (pp. 84–130). Basingstoke, Hampshire: Palgrave Macmillan.
Holt, M., Anderson, L., and Rouzie, A. (2003). Making emotion work visible in writing program administration. In D. Jacobs and L. R. Micciche (eds). *A way to move: Rhetorics of emotion and composition studies* (pp. 147–60). Portsmouth NH: Boynton/Cook.
Horowitz, E. (2001). Language anxiety and achievement. *Annual Review of Applied Linguistics 21*, 112–27.
Hughes, L. (1951). *Montage of a dream deferred*. New York: Holt.
In-Between Days (2007), dir. So Yong Kim. New York: Kino.
Jacobs, D. and Micciche, L. R. (eds) (2003). *A way to move: Rhetorics of emotion and composition studies*. Portsmouth NH: Boynton/Cook.
Johnson, K. E. (2006). The sociocultural turn and its challenges for second language teacher education. *TESOL Quarterly 40*, 235–50.
Johnson, K. E. and Golombek, P. R. (2002). Inquiry into experience: Teachers' personal and professional growth. In K. E. Johnson and P. R. Golombek (eds). *Teachers' narrative inquiry as professional development* (pp. 1–11). Cambridge: Cambridge University Press.
——(2003) "Seeing" teachers learning. *TESOL Quarterly 37*, 729–37.
Kramsch, C. (2003). Metaphor and the subjective construction of belief. In A. M. Barcelos and P. Kalaja (eds). *New approaches to research on beliefs about SLA* (pp. 109–28). Amsterdam: Kluwer Academic Publishing.
——(2008). Emotions in the cross-fire: Structuralist vs. post-structuralist stances in bilingualism research. *Bilingualism, Language, and Cognition 11*, 177–79.
——(2009). *The multilingual subject*. Oxford: Oxford University Press.
Krashen, S. D. (1982). *Principles and practice in second language acquisition*. Oxford: Pergamon.
Kumaravadivelu, B. (2003). *Beyond methods: Macrostrategies for language teaching*. New Haven: Yale University Press.
Leavitt, J. (1996). Meaning and feeling in the anthropology of emotions. *American Ethnologist 23*, 514–39.
Levy, B. (2000). Pedagogy: Incomplete, unrequited. In O'Farrell et al. (eds). *Taught bodies* (pp. 81–90). New York: Peter Lang.
Lo, A. (2009). Lessons about respect and affect in a Korean heritage language school. *Linguistics and Education 20*, 217–34.
Luke, A. (2004). Two takes on the critical. In B. Norton and K. Toohey (eds). *Critical pedagogies and language learning* (pp. 21–29). Cambridge: Cambridge University Press.
Luke, C. (2003). Pedagogy, connectivity, multimodality, and interdisciplinarity. *Reading Research Quarterly, 38*, 397–403.

——(2007). As seen on TV or was that my phone? *New Media literacy. Policy Futures in Education* 5, 50–58.
Mani-Pedis Go Green (www.hyphenmagazine.com/magazine/issue-18-action/mani-pedis-go-green).
Massumi, B. (2002). *Parables for the virtual: Movement, affect, sensation.* Durham NC: Duke University Press.
McWilliams, E. (1996). Admitting impediments: Or things to do with bodies in the classroom. *Cambridge Journal of Education* 26, 367–79.
——(2000). Stuck in the missionary position? Pedagogy and desire in new times. In O'Farrell et al. (eds). *Taught bodies* (pp. 27–37). New York: Peter Lang.
Meurant, R. C. (2008). The key importance of L2 digital literacy to Korean EFL pedagogy: College students use L2 English to make campus video guides with their cell phone videocams, and to view and respond to their videos on an L2 English language social networking site. *International Journal of Hybrid Information Technology* Vol. 1, No. 1. Retrieved from www.sersc.org/journals/IJHIT/vol1_no1_2008/IJHIT-Vol.1-No.1%20-%20The%20Key%20Importance%20of%20L2%20Digital%20Literacy%20to%20Korean%20EFL%20Pedagogy.pdf
Micciche, L. R. (2002). More than a feeling: Disappointment and WPA work. *College English* 64, 432–58.
——(2007). *Doing emotion: Rhetoric, writing, teaching.* Portsmouth NH: Boynton/Cook.
Misson, R. and Morgan, W. (2000). Teaching an embodied aesthetic: Towards a different practice in English. In O'Farrell et al. (eds). *Taught bodies.* (pp. 91–104). New York: Peter Lang.
Moody, A. (1968). *Coming of age in Mississippi.* New York: Dial Press.
Moore, C. and Shulock, N. (2007) *Beyond the open door: Increasing student success in the California community colleges.* Sacramento, CA: Institute for Higher Education Leadership and Policy.
Morgan, B. (2009). Fostering transformative practitioners for critical EAP: Possibilities and challlenges. *Journal of English for academic purposes* 8, 86–99.
Morgan, M. L. (ed.). (2006). *The essential Spinoza: Ethics and related writings.* Indianapolis: Hackett Publishing Company.
Ngai, S. (2005). *Ugly feelings.* Cambridge, MA: Harvard University Press.
Norton, B. (2000). *Identity and language learning: Gender, ethnicity and educational change.* Harlow: Pearson Educational.
On Campus (2005). Should colleges be allowed to bar military recruiters? November.
Oxford, R. L. (1999). Anxiety and the language learner: New insights. In J. Arnold (ed.). *Affect in language learning* (pp. 58–67). New York: Cambridge University Press.
Pavlenko, A. (2005). *Emotions and multilingualism.* Cambridge: Cambridge University Press.
Pavlenko, A. (ed.). (2006). *Bilingual minds: Emotional experience, expression, and representation.* Clevedon: Multilingual Matters.
Pennycook. A. (2001). *Critical applied linguistics: A critical introduction.* Mahwah NJ: Lawrence Erlbaum.
Prior, M. T. (2011). Self-presentation in L2 interview talk: Narrative versions, accountability, and emotionality. *Applied Linguistics* 32/1, 60–76.
Probyn, E. (2004). Teaching bodies: Affects in the classroom. *Body & Society* 10, 21–43.
Ryden, W. (2003). Conflict and kitsch: The politics of politeness in the writing class. In D. Jacobs and L. R. Micciche (eds). *A way to move: Rhetorics of emotion and composition studies* (pp. 80–91). Portsmouth NH: Boynton/Cook.
Schumann, J. H. (1999). A neurobiological perspective on affect and methodology in second language learning. In J. Arnold (ed.). *Affect in language learning* (pp. 28–42). New York: Cambridge University Press.
Starfield, S. (2004). "Why does this feel empowering?" Thesis writing, concordancing, and the corporatizing university. In B. Norton and K. Toohey (eds). *Critical pedagogies and language learning* (pp. 138–57). Cambridge: Cambridge University Press.

Stevick, E. (1999). Affect in learning and memory: From alchemy to chemistry. In J. Arnold (ed.). *Affect in language learning* (pp. 43–57). New York: Cambridge University Press.
Single White Female (1992), dir. Barbet Schroeder. New York: Columbia Pictures.
Ten Points to Consider Before You Sign a Military Enlistment Agreement (www.afsc.org/resources/documents/10pts-english.pdf).
TESOL Member Resolution on Granting Credit for ESL in Institutions of Higher Education (www.tesol.org/s_tesol/sec_document.asp?CID=87&DID=231).
The New Yorker's Guide to Military Recruitment (www.counterrecruitmentguide.org).
Thornton, P. and Houser, C. (2005). Using mobile phones in English education in Japan. *Journal of Computer Assisted Learning, 21*, 217–28.
Vandrick, S. (2009). *Interrogating privilege: Reflections of a second language educator.* Ann Arbor: The University of Michigan Press.
Verity, D. P. (2000). Side effects: The strategic development of professional satisfaction. In J. P. Lantolf (ed.). *Sociocultural theory and second language learning* (pp. 179–97). Oxford: Oxford University Press.
Washington Post. Army guard refilling its ranks: Members get bonus for new recruits. Mar. 12, 2006; A01.
Watkins, M. (2006). Pedagogic affect/effect: Embodying a desire to learn. *Pedagogies: An International Journal 1*, 269–82.
Worsham, L. (1998). Going postal: Pedagogic violence and the schooling of emotion. *Journal of Advanced Composition 18*, 213–45.
Zembylas, M. (2005) *Teaching with emotion: A postmodern enactment.* Greenwich CT: Information Age Publishing.
——(2007a). Theory and methodology in researching emotions in education. *International Journal of Research & Method in Education 10*, 57–72.
——(2007b). Emotional capital and education: Insights from Bourdieu. *British Journal of Educational Studies 55*, 443–63.

INDEX

"absent-presence" 4
admission policies 110; at CUNY 14–17, 18; open 14, 17, 18
aesthetics, embodied 91
affect 8, 24–6, 50, 113; autonomy of 39–41, 42–3; and cognition 22, 27, 57; critical teaching of 18, 31–2, 37–9, 48–53, 90–2; critical theorists 38–41; definitions of 22, 40, 77; Deleuzian notion of 8, 36, 38–9, 42; and dualism 38; and friendship 86; and group dynamics 24; and language learning 7–8, 21–4, 52–3, 90–2; origin in the mind 22; pedagogy of 77–8; as presocial 42; and social structures 22, 42; *vs.* emotions 21, 37–43, 132–4, 138
affective cycle 42
affective dimension 24, 76–7, 85–6
affective filter 6–7
affective problems 23
affective turn 37–43
affectivity 8, 9; dynamics of 49, 86
Ahmed, S. 5, 10, 21, 43; on affect and emotions 41–2; on happiness 46–8, 60–1; happy migrants 126–7; "inside out model" 21, 22, 26, 29; on migration 46–8; "outside in model" 26, 29; on ranking of emotions 5; on sticky objects 5, 57–8, 60–1, 62–3, 67
AL. *See* applied linguistics
Albrecht-Crane, C.: on affective dimension 85–6; on emotions 48, 49–50; on pedagogy 76, 77, 78

Albrecht-Crane, C. and Stack, J. D. 77–8, 85
anger 21, 23, 118, 124
anti-war movement 11–12, 79, 89
anxiety 60, 97–8; "language anxiety" 23; in language teaching 5–8, 9, 21–3, 25, 27
applied linguistics (AL) 32
Armed Forces, US 78–9, 81
Arnold, J. 7, 21
Arnold, J. and Brown, H. D. 7–8, 21, 22, 24
assessment tests 18, 110, 128, 137; emotional impact of 120–1
assignments, in class 51, 73, 95–101, 130, 131
asylum seekers 60
attachment: of emotions 57; to past 47–8; to sticky object 68–72
"attentive silence" 33
audiolingualism 13

becoming 39, 51, 78, 122; concept of 38
Bend it Like Beckham (film) 47–8
Benesch, S. 3–4, 15, 77, 79, 87, 137
Berkeley, University of California 31, 101
Berlant, L. 38, 44–6, 126, 138
bilingualism 28, 29
body 39, 40–3, 91–2; biomediated 40; in classrooms 115–7, 129, 136; embodiment of emotions 31, 36; language 91, 102, 117, 123–5, 126; and movement 40–1; relationship with

mind 21, 30–1, 42, 52, 94, 133; separation from mind 37–8; socialized 42; without organs 39
bodymaps 31
Boler, M. 4–5
Braidotti, R. 39
brain 21, 23, 31
British Empire 46
Brown, C. 17

CAL. *See* critical applied linguistics
Canada 9, 24, 32–3
Cantonese 32–3
cellphones: as instructional resource 73–4; as sticky objects 48, 58, 68–74; students' view of 70–4; teachers' view of 68–70; use of 72–4
children: emotional literacy 21; language use choices 33–4; and multilingualism 33
Chun, C. W. 109
City University of New York (CUNY) 14–15; admission policies 14–17, 18
Clarke, M. 13–14
Clough, P. T. 39–40, 42
cognition 6, 7; and affect 22, 27, 57; and emotions 22, 26; and language learning 20, 22, 34–5, 36, 94
Colebrook, C. 39, 40
College of Staten Island (CSI) 14
colleges, US: admission policies 14–17, 18; and military recruitment 76–85
Combination Platter (film) 95–6
compassion 44–5, 120, 123, 125
"compassionate conservatism" 44–5
contagion 116–7, 122–3
counter-recruitment material 79, 88
critical applied linguistics (CAL): and emotions 32, 34, 36; "struggle" 36; vs. applied linguistics 32
criticality 8
critical literacy 74–5
critical praxis 43–4, 48, 52, 79
critical teaching 79; of affect and emotions 18, 31–2, 37–9, 48–53, 86, 87; implications of research 130–4; and sticky objects 67–8, 72–4
critical theory 44, 49; the "affective turn" 37–43
culture 22–3, 30, 47–8; cross-cultural factors 22, 125; politics 5
CUNY. *See* City University of New York

Damasio, A. 31, 36
Das Kurze Leben des José Antonio Gutierrez (The Short Life of José Antonio Gutierrez) (film) 88
Davies, B. et al. 131
Deleuze, G. 8, 38–9, 40, 42, 77, 92; "becoming" 38, 39, 51, 78, 122; body without organs 39; lines of flight 39, 49, 50, 77–8, 133
Deleuze, G. and Guattari, F. 39
Deleuzian: approach 49, 50, 77, 117; notion of affect 8, 36, 38–9, 42
desire 50–1, 77–8, 116
dialogue 49, 92
dictionaries: on cellphones 73–4; as commodities 75; as sticky objects 61–8; teachers' view of 64–7; use of 58, 62–3, 65–7, 74
disappointment 61–8
discourses 9, 29, 46, 51, 118; of difference 50; of dissent and protest 11, 17; of emotion 135; of partiality 4
dissonance, emotional 26, 27, 35
Dornyei, Z. and Malderez, A. 24
dualism 38

educational institutions: post-secondary 109, 110 *See also* colleges, US
ELT. *See* English language teaching
embodiment 32, 34, 36, 44, 99, 133–4; bodies in the classroom 115–7, 129, 136; as contagion 122–3; embodied aesthetic pedagogy 91; embodied self 30–2; relationship to metaphors 101–3, 104–5; of responses 90–2; teachers' in-class emotions 122–6, 129
emotional affinities 52, 115, 129
emotional competence 24
emotional intelligence 21, 35
emotional labor *see* emotion work
emotional literacy 21, 134–5
emotional rules 51, 52, 114–5
emotion management 118–121
emotions: "absent-presence" 4; "appropriate" 112, 118–9, 129; categories of 21, 43, 94, 133; cognitive approaches in ELT 20, 22, 26, 34–5; conceptualization of 27, 28–9, 31, 35–6; and critical applied linguistics 32, 34, 36; critical teaching of 18, 31–2, 48–53, 86, 87; and ELTs 5–7, 48, 51–3, 110–129; explicit teaching of 125–6; in language learning 7–8, 20–4, 29, 30–2,

34–5, 53, 94, 95, 97–9, 100, 107; and multilingualism 27–30; negative 7–8, 21, 23–4, 34–5, 126; and objects 47–8, 57–75; positive 7–8, 21, 23–4, 34–5, 59; and power 5, 32–4, 36, 44; private vs social vii, 8, 10, 29, 44, 126, 133, 135; relativist theory of 28–9; and sticky objects 5, 52, 57–75, 133; of teachers in class 122–6, 129; universalist theory of 28–9; *vs.* affect 21, 37–43, 132–4, 138; vs feelings 31, 41, 43, 44
emotion words 27, 28, 35, 96
emotion work 109–129; "appropriate emotions" 112, 118–20; body language 91, 102, 117, 123–5, 126; contagion 116–7, 122–3; ugly feelings 42, 126–9
English language teaching (ELT) 21; critical ELT 5, 8–10, 90, 92, 126; teacher emotions 110–111; see *also* language teaching
envy 43, 44–6
Erhmann, M. 21
ESL (English as a Second Language) 64, 68–71; and admission policies 14–16, 128; classes 65–71, 80, 88, 111, 123; at CUNY 16–7
excitement 51, 91
"expanded mandate" 21

family: attachment to 69, 71–2; "happy family" 60–1
fast-track citizenship 78
feelings: minor 43; negative 8, 35; ugly 43, 126–9; vs emotions 31, 41, 43, 44
feminism: feminist scholarship 41, 43–48, 112; feminist theories 4, 8; and poststructuralism 45–6
films 45–6, 47–8, 88, 95–6
foreign language learning. *See* language learning
Freeman, D. and Johnson, K. 25
Freire, P. 14, 16
French 30–1
Freshman Workshop Program (FWP) 15
friendship 49, 85, 86, 92; pedagogy of 78, 88–90, 92
frustration 4, 23, 67, 100, 102, 106, 119, 120, 121

Gattegno, C. 12–14
globalization 32, 34
Goldstein, T. 32–4
Goleman, D. 21, 23

Golombek, P. R. and Johnson, K. E. 25–7
"goosebump effect" 91, 92
Gorton, K. 6
Granger, C. A. 138
Great Society 44–5
Grey, M. 50–1, 52, 73
Griffin, J. H. 17
group dynamics 24, 45
Gubar, S. 46

Hague, William 60
happiness 46–8; crisis 61; "happy family" 60–1; "happy migrant" 47, 127; maximization of 47
Hardt, M. 37
Hargreaves, A. 113
Harwood, N. 138
Harris, O. 58–9
Hemmings, C. 42–3
Hochschild, A. 109, 112–4
Hoffman, E. 23–4
Holoborow, M. 110
Holt, M., Anderson, L., and Rouzie, A. 113–4
Horowtiz, E. 21
hope 61–8
Hughes, L. 17
humanists 7, 115, 116

identity 9, 32, 76–7, 78, 86, 120; constructions 40
immigrants 95–101, 128, 135; in Canada 9–10, 32–4; happiness of 47; language problems of 67, 71–2; media portrayals of 46; and military recruitment 78–9, 87–8; students 32–4, 63, 67, 73, 78
In-Between Days (film) 95–6
indignation 85
inequality and envy 45
"inside out" model of emotions 21, 22, 26, 29
"interiority" (presumption of) 21
Iraq 78, 79, 88

Jacobs, D. and Micciche, L. R. 113
Johnson, K. E. and Golombek, P. R. 25

Kramsch, C. 20, 29–32, 36, 94; on metaphors 101–4, 106, 108; on multilingualism 30, 36; on second language acquisition 94–5
Krashen, S. 6–7
Kumaravadivelu, B. 93, 95

LAD (Language Acquisition Device) 7
language acquisition *see* language learning
language choices 33
language learning 23–4, 28–31, 94–5; and affect 7–8, 21–4, 52–3, 90–2; cognitive approaches to 7–8, 20–1, 34–5, 94; and critical applied linguistics 32; cross-cultural factors 22–3; embodied self 30–2, 107; emotional attachment to languages 28–9, 33–4; emotions in 7–9, 20–4, 29, 53, 94–5, 97–9, 100, 107; and identity 30, 103; LAD (Language Acquisition Device) 7; language anxiety 23; metaphors for 31–32, 101–8, 134; physical aspects of 30–1; the Silent Way 12–14, 137. see also language teaching
language teachers: care towards students 7, 119; on cellphone use in class 68–70; on classroom behavior 24, 119; on dictionary use in class 64–7; education of 25–7; and emotion work 110–125; in-class emotions 122–6, 129; leadership styles 24; role of 7, 8, 24, 115–6; views of 25, 26
language teaching 12–13, 133; anxiety 23; cognitive approaches to 35, 36; and critical applied linguistics 32; decision-making in 51–2; dictionaries 62–8; emotions in 5, 7, 30, 51–3, 110–; ESL 14–16; narratives 25–7; research 28–9, 32, 50, 51, 62–8; the Silent Way 12–14; sociocultural approaches to 25–7, 35; and sticky objects 57–8, 67–8; student feedback 26; "temporary other" 25–7; traditional goals of 30, 52, 95; visceral reactions in 92, 134
language theories 68
laziness 62–4
leadership styles 24
learning outcomes: predefined 116
Leavitt, J. 37, 38
Levy, B. 115
"lines of flight" 39, 49, 50, 77–8, 133
linguistic change 74
literacy tests 14, 16, 35, 120–1; emotional effect of 18, 120
Lo, A. 34, 36
Luke, A. 8–9, 10
Luke, C. 74

Massumi, B. 39, 40–1, 42
McWilliams, E. 115–6
meaning-making, symbolic 31

melancholia 47
metaphors for language learning 31–2, 101–8, 134; of paradox 104, 105–7; research on 101–8
Meurant, R. C. 73
Micciche, L. R. 113, 129
migrants: and happiness 47, 126–7; melancholic 46–7
military recruitment 76–92; counter-recruiter 88–90; emotional response to 85–6; socio-historical background 78–9; students' views on 80–4
Mills, James 47
mind 21–2, 40, 49, 94; relationship with body 21, 30–1, 42, 52, 94, 133
Misson, R. and Morgan, W. 90–1
molar lines 77, 78
monolingualism 33
Moody, A. 17
Moore, C. and Shulock, N. 137
Morgan, B. 10
Morgan, M. L. 38
motivation 6, 7, 9, 100, 116
movement 40, 41
multidisciplinary approach to emotions 27, 35–6
multilingualism 27, 29–30, 33, 36, 95; students with non-English-speaking relatives 71–2

narratives 25–7
negative emotions 7–8, 21, 23–4, 34–5, 126
neoliberalism 110, 115–6, 127–8, 135, 138
Ngai, S. 39, 42–3, 45
nomadic ethnographers 50
Norton, B. 9–10

objects: and emotions 47–8, 57–75; intangible 60, 61; sticky 57–75
"outside in" model of emotions 27, 29
Oxford, R. L. 23

pain 18, 31, 102, 121; physical 30, 91; social 45
Pavlenko, A. 27–9, 35–6
pedagogic affect 116–7
pedagogy 49, 51, 67, 76; of affect 77; of friendship 78, 88–90, 92; out-of-class 73–4
"peer social capital" 33
Pennycook, A. 32

politics 18, 44, 128; cultural 5, 58
positive emotions 7–8, 21, 23–4, 34–5, 59
poststructuralism 29, 40, 42, 44, 49; assumptions of identity and power 39; and feminism 46
power: and emotions 5, 32–4, 36, 44
"presumption of interiority" 21
Prior, M. T. 138
Probyn, E. 90–2, 115, 117, 134
proficiency tests 14, 94
psycholinguistics 93–4

questionnaires 58, 62–3

racism 47–8, 83
research: questionnaires 58, 62–3
resentment 68–74, 110
resignation 99, 121
Ryden, W. 90

Schumann, J. H. 23–4
second language acquisition 6–7, 93–4, 99–100; and emotions 107; Language Acquisition Device (LAD) 7; as symbolic system 94; theories 93–4; *see also* language learning
self: embodied 30–2; "self-othering" 9
self-esteem 116, 135
Silent Way 12–14, 137
Single White Female (film) 45–6
SLA. *See* second language acquisition
social change 10–11, 17
social contexts 34–5, 112
social/emotional history 10–11, 14–17
social structures 22, 42
social vs. cognitive approach 22, 34
socio-cultural approaches to teacher education 35
Spinoza, B. 38–41
Starfield, S. 110
Stevick, E. 21
"sticky objects" 5, 57–75, 133–4; attachment to 68–72; cellphones 48, 58, 68–74; dictionaries 61–8; implications for critical teaching 67–8, 72–4; intangible 60, 61
"struggle" in critical applied linguistics 36
student feedback 26

students, diasporic 4, 34, 108
student/teacher relationship 7, 49–50, 51, 85, 86, 92, 123; and body language 127–8, 135; pedagogic affect 116; treatment of ugly feelings 127–8, 135
subject positions 40, 46
"surfaces" 58
symbolic meaning-making 31
symbolic systems 30, 92, 134

tea, associations with 59–60
"teacher-learners" 25, 86
teachers. *See* language teachers
teacher/student relationship 7, 49–50, 51, 85, 86, 92, 123; and body language 123–4; pedagogic affect 116; treatment of ugly feelings 127–8, 135
teaching materials: counter-recruitment 77, 79, 88–9; ELT 77, 92, 118, 124; Silent Way 12
technology: electronic dictionaries 75; impact of 40; and linguistic change 74 *See also* cellphones
testing 14–16; assessment tests 110, 120–1, 128
The Promise of Happiness 46–8
Thornton, P. and Houser, C. 73

ugly feelings 43, 126–9
unhappiness 34–5, 48, 61, 127, 128
universalist theories 28–9
University of California, Berkeley 31, 101
utilitarianism 46–7

Vandrick, S. 59–61, 137
Verity, D. P. 26
vocabulary: extending 61–2, 73–5; and linguistic change 74

Washington, March on 11, 17
Watkins, M. 116–7, 122
Wiegman, R. 46
Worsham, L. 109
WPA (writing program administrators) 113–5

Zembylas, M. 51–2, 114–5, 129, 135, 138; list of teacher emotions 111